S.G.W. Benjamin

Art in America

A critical and historical sketch

S.G.W. Benjamin

Art in America
A critical and historical sketch

ISBN/EAN: 9783337012953

Printed in Europe, USA, Canada, Australia, Japan

Cover: Foto ©ninafisch / pixelio.de

More available books at **www.hansebooks.com**

A CRITICAL AND HISTORICAL SKETCH

BY

S. G. W. BENJAMIN

AUTHOR OF "CONTEMPORARY ART IN EUROPE" "WHAT IS ART" &c.

ILLUSTRATED

NEW YORK
HARPER & BROTHERS, PUBLISHERS
FRANKLIN SQUARE
1880

Entered according to Act of Congress, in the year 1879, by

HARPER & BROTHERS,

In the Office of the Librarian of Congress, at Washington.

ERRATUM.

The cut on page 28, attributed to Rembrandt Peale, should be credited to John T. Peele.

PREFACE.

The aim of this book has been to give a historical outline of the growth of the arts in America. But while this has been the dominating idea in the mind of the writer, criticism has necessarily entered, more or less, into the preparation of the work, since only by weighing the differences or the comparative merits of those artists who seemed best to illustrate the various phases of American art has it been possible to trace its progress from one step to another.

It is from no lack of appreciation of their talents that the author has apparently neglected mention of the American artists resident in foreign capitals — like Bridgman, Duveneck, Wight, Neal, Bacon, Benson, Ernest Parton, Millet, Whistler, Dana, Blashfield, Miss Gardner, Miss Conant, and many others who have done credit to American æsthetic culture. But it was necessary to draw the line somewhere; and to discuss what our artists are painting abroad would have at once enlarged the scope of the work beyond the limits of the plan adopted. An exception has been made in the case of our sculptors, because they have so uniformly lived and wrought in Europe, and so large a proportion of them are still resident there, that, were we to confine this branch of the subject only to the sculptors now actually in America, there would be little left to say about their department of our arts.

The author takes this occasion cordially to thank the artists and amateurs who have kindly permitted copies of their paintings and drawings to be engraved for this volume.

CONTENTS.

ILLUSTRATIONS.

SUBJECT.	ARTIST.	PAGE
PORTRAIT OF A LADY	John Singleton Copley	Frontispiece
FAMILY OF BISHOP BERKELEY	John Smybert	16
DEATH ON THE PALE HORSE	Benjamin West	19
DEATH OF MONTGOMERY	John Trumbull	23
GENERAL KNOX	Gilbert Stuart	25
"BEGGAR'S OPERA"	G. Stuart Newton	27
"BABES IN THE WOOD"	Rembrandt Peale	28
FANNY KEMBLE	Thomas Sully	29
ARIADNE	John Vanderlyn	30
THE HOURS	E. G. Malbone	32
JEREMIAH	Washington Allston	34
DYING HERCULES	Samuel F. B. Morse	35
"MUMBLE THE PEG"	Henry Inman	40
PORTRAIT OF PARKE GODWIN	Thomas Le Clear	43
PORTRAIT OF FLETCHER HARPER	C. L. Elliott	45
AN IDEAL HEAD	G. A. Baker	48
THE JUDGMENT OF PARIS	Henry Peters Grey	50
MIRANDA	Daniel Huntington	53
A SURPRISE	William Sidney Mount	55
TAKING THE VEIL	Robert Weir	57
DESOLATION. FROM "THE COURSE OF EMPIRE"	Thomas Cole	59
A STUDY FROM NATURE	A. B. Durand	61
NOON BY THE SEA-SHORE.—BEVERLY BEACH	J. F. Kensett	63
ALTORF, BIRTH-PLACE OF WILLIAM TELL	George L. Brown	64
BROOK IN THE WOODS	Worthington Whittredge	67
LANDSCAPE COMPOSITION	R. W. Hubbard	70
"THE VASTY DEEP"	William T. Richards	72
HIGH TORN, ROCKLAND LAKE	Jasper F. Cropsey	74
THE PARSONAGE	A. F. Bellows	75
LANDSCAPE WITH CATTLE	James Hart	77
SUNSET ON THE HUDSON	Sandford R. Gifford	80
A COMPOSITION	Frederick E. Church	82
A WINTER SCENE	Louis R. Mignot	84
SHIP OF "THE ANCIENT MARINER"	James Hamilton	85
"WHOO!"	William H. Beard	87
LAFAYETTE IN PRISON	E. Leutze	89
PORTRAIT OF A LADY	William Page	91
THE REFUGE	Elihu Vedder	93
CARTOON SKETCH: CHRIST AND NICODEMUS	John Lafarge	95
VIEW ON THE KERN RIVER	A. Bierstadt	99
THE YOSEMITE	Thomas Hill	100
THE BATHERS	Thomas Moran	101
LANDSCAPE	Jervis McEntee	104
COUNTY KERRY	A. H. Wyant	105
THE ADIRONDACKS	Homer Martin	107

ILLUSTRATIONS.

SUBJECT.	ARTIST.	PAGE
A Landscape	J. W. Casilear	109
Ship Ashore	M. F. H. De Haas	111
A Foggy Morning	W. E. Norton	112
A Marine	Arthur Quartley	114
Arguing the Question	T. W. Wood	116
The Rose	B. F. Mayer	118
Dress Parade	J. G. Brown	120
A Bed-time Story	S. J. Guy	121
The Mother	Eastman Johnson	123
Sail-boat	Winslow Homer	124
The Scout	Wordsworth Thompson	126
On the Old Sod	William Magrath	127
"A Matin Song"	Fidelia Bridges	129
Study of a Dog	Frank Rogers	130
Lost in the Snow	A. F. Tait	132
Eve before the Fall	Hiram Powers	135
Orpheus	Thomas Crawford	137
Columbus before the Council. From the Bronze Door of the Capitol at Washington	Randolph Rogers	139
The Ghost in "Hamlet"	Thomas R. Gould	141
George Washington	J. Q. A. Ward	143
Medea	William Wetmore Story	146
The Promised Land	Franklin Simmons	147
Latona and her Infants	W. H. Rinehart	150
Zenobia	Harriet Hosmer	152
Evening	E. D. Palmer	153
Bust of William Page	William R. O'Donovan	155
Abraham Pierson	Launt Thompson	157
The Charity Patient	John Rogers	158
The Whirlwind	J. S. Hartley	159
Adoration of the Cross by Angels. St. Thomas's Church, New York	Augustus St. Gaudens	160
Thomas Jefferson's Idea of a Monument		162
The Mowing	Alfred Fredericks	165
Birds in the Forest	Miss Jessie Curtis	169
Representing the Manner of Peter's Courtship	Howard Pyle	171
Some Art Connoisseurs	W. Hamilton Gibson	173
Washington opening the Ball	C. S. Reinhart	175
Museum of Fine Arts, Boston		178
The Astonished Abbé	E. A. Abbey	181
A Child's Portrait	B. C. Porter	184
A Bit of Venice	Samuel Colman	185
The Old Orchard	R. Swain Gifford	187
A Landscape	George Inness	188
La Marguerette—the Daisy	William M. Hunt	189
Moonlight	John J. Enneking	191
Having a Good Time	Louis C. Tiffany	192
Southampton, Long Island	C. H. Miller	193
A Study	Frederick Dielman	195
The Burgomaster	H. Muhrman	197
Burial of the Dead Bird	J. Alden Weir	200
The Apprentice	William M. Chase	201
The Professor	Thomas Eakins	204
The Goose-herd	Walter Shirlaw	205
A Spanish Lady	Mary S. Cassatt	208
Study of a Boy's Head	W. Sartain	209

ART IN AMERICA.

I.

EARLY AMERICAN ART.

THE art of a nation is the result of centuries of growth; its crowning excellence does not come except when maturity and repose offer the occasion for its development. But while, therefore, it is yet too soon to look for a great school of art in America, the time has perhaps arrived to note some of the preliminary phases of the art which, we have reason to hope, is to dawn upon the country before long.

As the heirs of all the ages, we had a right to expect that our intellectual activity would demand art expression; while the first efforts would naturally be imitative rather than original. The individuality which finds vent in the utterance of truth under new conditions is not fully reached until youth gives place to the vigorous self-assertion of a manhood conscious of its resources and power. Such we find to have been the case in the rise of the fine arts in this country, which up to this time have been rather an echo of the art of the lands from which our ancestors came, than distinctively original. Our art has been the result of affectionate remembrance of foreign achievement more than of independent observation of nature; and while the number of artists has been sufficiently large, very few of them stand forth as representatives or types of novel methods and ideas; and those few, coming before their time, have met with little response in the community, and their influence has been generally local and moderate, leading to the founding of nothing like a school except in one or two isolated cases. But many of them, especially in the first period of our art, have shared the strong, active character of their time;

and, like the heroes of the Revolution, presented sturdy traits of character. And thus, while the society in which they moved was not sufficiently advanced to appreciate the quality of their art, they were yet able to stamp their names indelibly upon the pages of our history. But within the last few years the popular interest in art has grown so rapidly in the country —as indicated by the establishment of numerous art schools and academies, art galleries, and publications treating exclusively of art subjects, together with many other significant proofs of concern in the subject—that it seems safe to assume that the first preparatory period of American art, so brilliant in many respects, is about closing, and that we are now on the threshold of another, although it is only scarcely three centuries since the first English colonists landed on our shores. The first professional artist of whom there seems to be any record in our colonial history was possessor of a title that does not often fall to the lot of the artist: he was a deacon. This fact indicates that Deacon Shem Drowne, of Boston town, was not only a cunning artificer in metals and wood-carving, as the old chronicles speak of him, but also a man addicted to none of the small vices that are traditionally connected with the artistic career; for people were very proper in that vicinage in those days of austere virtue and primness, and deacons were esteemed the very salt of the earth.

During the first century of our colonial existence local painters, often scarcely deserving the name, are also known to have gained a precarious livelihood by taking meagre portraits of the worthies of the period, in black and white or in color. We should know this to have been the fact by the portraits—quaint, and often rude and awkward—which have come down to us, without anything about them to indicate who the artists could have been who painted them. Occasionally a suggestion of talent is evident in those canvases from which the stiff ruffles and bands of the Puritans stare forth at us. Cotton Mather also alludes to a certain artist whom he speaks of as a limner. But in those times there was, however, at best no art in this country, except what was brought over occasionally in the form of family portraits, painted by Vandyck, Rembrandt, Lely, or Kneller. These precious heirlooms, scarcely appreciated by the stern theologians of the time, were, however, not without value in advancing the cause of civilization among the wilds of the Western world. Unconsciously the minds of coming generations were influenced and moulded by these reminders of the great art of other lands and ages. No human effort is wasted; somewhere, at some time, it appears, as the seed sown in October comes forth anew in April, quickened into other forms, to sustain life under fresh conditions.

The first painter in America of any decided ability whose name has survived to this day was John Watson, who executed portraits in Philadelphia in 1715. He was a Scotchman. It is to another Scotchman, who married and identified himself with the rising fortunes of the colonies, that we are perhaps able to assign the first distinct and decided art impulse in this country. And for this we are directly indebted to Bishop Berkeley, whose sagacious eye penetrated so far through the mists of futurity, and realized the coming greatness of the land.

Berkeley is associated with the literature and arts of America in several ways. He aided the advance of letters by a grant of books to Yale College, and by founding the nucleus of what later became the Redwood Library at Newport; thus indirectly suggesting architectural beauty to a people without examples of it, for in 1750 a building was erected for the library that sprang from his benefactions. The design was obtained from Vanbrugh, one of the greatest architects of modern times; and although the little library is constructed only of wood and mortar, its plan is so pleasing, tasteful, and harmonious, that it long remained the most graceful structure in the colonies; and even at this day is scarcely equalled on the continent as a work of art by many far more costly and ambitious constructions after the Renaissance order. And, finally, we owe to Bishop Berkeley the most notable impulse which the dawning arts received in this country when he induced John Smybert, the Scotchman, to leave London in 1725 and settle in Boston, where he had the good fortune to marry a rich widow, and lived prosperous and contented until his death, in 1751. Smybert was not a great painter. If he had remained in Europe his position never would have been more than respectable, even at an age when the arts were at a low ebb. But he is entitled to our gratitude for perpetuating for us the lineaments of many worthies of the period, and for the undoubted impetus his example gave to the artists who were about to come on the scene and assert the right of the New World to exercise its energies in the encouragement of the fine arts. It is by an apparently unimportant incident that the influence of Smybert to our early art is most vividly illustrated. He brought with him to America an excellent copy of a Vandyck, executed by himself; and several of our artists, including Allston, acknowledged that a sight of this copy affected them like an inspiration. The most important work of Smybert in this country is a group representing the family of Bishop Berkeley, now in the art gallery at New Haven. A flock of foreign portrait-painters, following the example of Smybert, now came over to this country, and rendered good service in perpetuating the faces of the notable characters and beauties of the time; but none of them were of special moment, excepting, perhaps, Blackburn and Alexander. But their labor bore fruit in preparing the way for the successes of Copley. The first native American

FAMILY OF BISHOP BERKELEY.—[JOHN SMYBERT.]

painter of merit of whom there is any authentic record was Robert Feke, who was of Quaker descent, and settled in Newport, where portraits of his are still to be seen, notably that of the beautiful wife of Governor Wanton, which is preserved in the Redwood Library. What little art-education he received resulted from his being taken prisoner at sea and carried to Spain, where he contrived to acquire a few hints in the use of pigments. Feke was a man of undoubted ability; and the same may be said of Matthew Pratt, of Philadelphia, who was born in 1734, in respect of age antedating both Copley and West, although not known until after they had acquired fame, because for many years he contented himself with the painting of signs and house decorations.

But the latent æsthetic capacity of the colonies displayed itself suddenly when John Singleton Copley, at the early age of seventeen, after only the most rudimentary instruction, adopted art as a profession. But, although a professional and successful artist at so early an age, Copley seems to have been preceded in assuming the calling of artist by a Quaker lad of Pennsylvania, one year his junior, but evincing a turn for art at an earlier age, when hardly out of the cradle.

The birth of a national art has scarcely ever been more affecting or remarkable than that recorded in the first efforts of Benjamin West. He was born at Springfield, Pennsylvania, in 1738, a year after Copley. The scientist of the future may perhaps show us that it was something more than a coincidence that the six leading painters of the first period of American art came in pairs: Copley and West in 1737 and 1738; Stuart and Trumbull were born in 1756; Vanderlyn arrived in 1776; and Allston followed only three years later.

The descendants of the iconoclasts who had beaten down statues and burned masterpieces of art, who had cropped their hair and passed sumptuary laws to fulfil the dictates of their creed, and had sought a wilderness across the seas where they could maintain their rigid doctrines unmolested, were now about to vindicate the character of their fathers. They were now to prove that the love of beauty is universal and unquenchable, and that sooner or later every people, kindred, and tongue seeks to utter its aspirations after the ideal good by art forms and methods; and that the sternness of the Puritans had been really directed, not so much against art and beauty legitimately employed, as against the abuse of the purest and noblest emotions of the soul by a debasing art.

As if to emphasize the truth of these observations, as well as of the famous prophecy of Bishop Berkeley, the artist to whom American art owes its rise, and for many years its greatest source of encouragement, was named West, and was of Quaker lineage. Such was the rude condition of the arts in the neighborhood at that time that the first initiation of West into art was as simple as that of Giotto. At nine years of age he drew hairs from a cat's tail and made himself a brush. Colors he obtained by grinding charcoal and chalk, and crushing the red blood out from the blackberry. His mother's laundry furnished him with indigo, and the friendly Indians who came to his father's house gave him of the red and yellow earths with which they daubed their faces. With such rude materials the lad painted a child sleeping in its cradle; and in that first effort of precocious genius executed certain touches which he never surpassed, as he affirmed long after, when at the zenith of his remarkable career.

How, from such primitive efforts, the Quaker youth gradually worked into local fame, went to Italy and acquired position there, and then settled in England, became the favorite *protégé* of the king for forty years, and the President of the National Academy of Great Britain—these are all matters of history, and, as West never forgot his love for his native land, entitle him to the respectful remembrance not only of artists, but of all his countrymen. American art has every reason, also, to cherish his memory with profound gratitude, for no painter ever conducted himself with greater kindness and generosity to the rising, struggling artists of his native land. No sooner did our early painters reach London but they resorted, for aid and guidance, to West, and found in him a friend who lent them his powerful influence without grudging, or allowed them to set up their easels in his studio, and gave them all the instruction in his power. Trumbull, Stuart, Dunlap, and many others, long after they had forgotten the natural foibles of West, had reason to remember how great had been the services he had rendered to the aspiring artists of his transatlantic home.

Since the death of West—whom we must consider one of the greatest men our country has produced—it has become the fashion to decry his art and belittle his character. This seems to be a mistake which reflects discredit upon his detractors. Men should be judged not absolutely, but relatively; not compared with perfection, but with their contemporaries and their opportunities. In estimating men of the past, also, we need to put ourselves in their places, rather than to regard them by the standard of the age in which we live. In no pursuit are men more likely to be misjudged than in art; for artists are liable to be guided by impulse rather than judgment, and the very vehemence of their likes and dislikes renders their opinions intense rather than broad and charitable. Benjamin West appears to have been born with great natural powers, which matured rapidly, and early ceased to develop in excellence proportionate to his extraordinary industry and fidelity to art.

But while a general evenness of quality rather than striking excellence in any particular works was the characteristic of the art of West, together with a certain brick-red tone in his colors not always agreeable, yet a share of genius must be granted to the artist who painted the "Departure

"DEATH ON THE PALE HORSE."—[BENJAMIN WEST.]

of Regulus," "Death on the Pale Horse," and "The Death of Wolfe." It unquestionably implied daring and consciousness of power to brave the opposition of contemporary opinions and abandon classic costume in historical compositions as he did; to win to his side the judgment of Sir Joshua Reynolds, and create a revolution in certain phases of art. Notwithstanding this, however, West was emphatically a man of his time, moulded by it rather than forming it, and inclined to conventionalism. When he entered the arena, art was in a depressed condition both in Italy, where he studied, and in England. But while Reynolds and Gainsborough gave a fresh impulse to art, West's genius, ripening precociously, early became incapable of achieving further progress.

West established himself as a portrait-painter at the age of fifteen; and in the following year—1755—Copley also engaged in the same pursuit, when only seventeen. The former lived to be seventy-nine; the latter was seventy-eight at his death. The art-life of Copley must be considered the most indigenous and strictly American of the two. Although receiving some early instruction from his step-father, Pelham, and enjoying opportunities denied to West, of studying portraits by foreign artists, yet Copley's advantages were excessively meagre; and whatever successes he achieved with his brush, until he finally settled in England at the age of thirty-nine, were entirely his own, and can be proudly included among the most valued treasures of our native art. So highly were the abilities of Copley esteemed in his day, that years before he crossed the Atlantic his reputation had preceded him, and assured him ready patronage in London.

It is said that Copley was a very slow and laborious worker. The elaboration he gave to the details of costume doubtless required time. But if the popular opinion was correct, we must assume that many of the paintings now reputed to be by his hand are spurious. It is a common saying that a Copley in a New England family is almost equivalent to a title of nobility; and this very fact would lead many to attribute to him family portraits by forgotten artists, who had, perhaps, caught the trick of his style. But there yet remain enough well authenticated portraits by this great painter, in excellent preservation, to render the study of his works one of great interest to the art student. There is no mistaking the handling of Copley. Self-taught, his merits and defects are entirely his own. His style was open to the charge of excessive dryness; the outlines are sometimes hard, and the figures stiff almost to ungracefulness. The last fault was, however, less noticeable in the formal, stately characters and costumes of the time than it would be under different conditions. In Copley's best compositions these errors are scarcely perceptible. He was far superior to West as a colorist, and was especially felicitous in catching the expression of the eye, and reproducing the elegant dress of the period; while we have had no artist who has excelled him in perceiving and interpreting the individuality and character of the hand. A very fine example of his skill in this respect is seen in the admirable portrait of Mrs. Relief Gill, taken when she was eighty years old. Gilbert Stuart remarked of the hand in the portrait of Colonel Epes Sargent, "Prick that hand, and blood will spurt out." It is indeed a masterpiece. No painter was ever more in sympathy with his age than Copley; and thus, when we look at the admirable portraits in which his genius commemorated the commanding characters of those colonial days, in their brilliant and massive uniforms, their brocades and embroidered velvets, and choice laces and scarfs, the imagination is carried back to the past with irresistible force, while, at the same time, we are astonished at the ability which, with so little training, could give immortality both to his contemporaries and his own pencil.

While the fame of Copley will ultimately rest on the masterly portraits which he bequeathed to posterity, yet it will not be forgotten that he was one of the ablest historical painters of his time. The compositions entitled the "Boy and the Squirrel," painted in Boston, the "Death of Major Pierson," and the "Death of Chatham," will contribute for ages to the fame of one of the most important American artists of the last century.

Charles Wilson Peale, the next artist of reputation in the colonies, owes his celebrity partly to accidental circumstances. Of course a certain degree of ability is implied in order that one may know how to turn the winds of fortune to the best account when they veer in his favor. But in some cases, as with Copley and West, man seems to wrest fate to his advantage; while in others she appears actually to throw herself in his way, and offer him opportunities denied to others. At any rate, it seems no injustice to ascribe the continued fame of Charles Wilson Peale to the fact that he was enabled to associate his art with the name of Washington; and that his son, Rembrandt, by also following art pursuits, was able to emphasize the fame of the family name. Peale the elder was not a specialist; he was rather, like so many born in America, gifted with a general versatility that enabled him to succeed moderately well in whatever he undertook, without achieving the highest excellence in any department. Inclining alternately to science and mechanics, he finally drifted into art, went over to England and studied with West, and returned to America in time to enter the army and rise to the rank of colonel. His versatile turn of mind is well illustrated by one who says that "he sawed his own ivory for his miniatures, moulded the glasses, and made the shagreen cases."

It was the good fortune of Peale to paint several excellent portraits of Washington, representing him during the military part of his career, both before and during the Revolution. Lacking many of the qualities of good art, these portraits are yet faithful and characteristic likenesses of the Father of his Country, and as such are of great interest and value.

It is to another Revolutionary soldier of superior natural ability, Colonel John Trumbull, that the country is indebted for a proof of the national turn for the fine arts. The son of Jonathan Trumbull, Colonial Governor of Connecticut, he received a classical education at Harvard

University. But here, again, observe the far-reaching influence of one act. That copy, already alluded to, which was executed by Smybert after a work of Vandyck—the great painter who was welcomed to the banqueting halls of merry England by Charles I. and Henrietta Maria—was again to bear fruit. It inspired the genius of Trumbull with a passion for color while yet in his youth, and ultimately led to his becoming a great historical painter.

But first he had to undergo the discipline of war, which gave him that experimental knowledge of which he afterward made such good use. Of a high spirit and proud, irascible temper, Trumbull served with distinction; first as aid to Washington, then as major at the storming of the works of Burgoyne at Saratoga; and he had reached a coloneley, when he threw up his commission and went over to England, and became a student of West, whose style is perceptible in many of the works of the younger artist.

If inequality is one sign of genius, then Trumbull possessed it to a marked degree. The difference in merit between his best paintings, which were chiefly composed in England, and those he executed in this country, in the later years of his life, is remarkable. This probably was due in part to the lack of any appreciable art influences or patronage in his own country to stimulate the artistic afflatus. The talents of Trumbull were conspicuous in portraiture and historical painting. The energy of his nature is illustrated in such powerful portraits as those of Washington and Hamilton. Deficient in drawing, and unlike in details of feature, they are life-like in their general resemblance, and seem to thrill with the spirit of the original. We see before us the heroes who conducted the struggling colonies successfully to military independence and political freedom. Trumbull's miniatures in oil of many of the men who were prominent in the Revolution are also very spirited and characteristic, and of inestimable historic value. He was less successful in the representation of feminine beauty. His talents moved within a limited range, but within that narrow circle displayed certain excellences quite rare in the Anglo-Saxon art of that period, exhibiting a correct feeling for color, keen perception of character, and great force of expression. But let him stray beyond the compass of his powers, as in the representation of woman, and his coloring becomes unnatural and his drawing inexpressive.

The art of this great painter, for so we must call him in view of some of his works, culminated in the historical compositions entitled "The Signing of the Declaration of Independence," "The Siege of Gibraltar," and the immortal compositions representing the "Death of Montgomery" and the "Battle of Bunker Hill." The last two were not surpassed by any similar works in the last century, and thus far stand alone in American historical painting.

Cabinet in size, they combine breadth and detail to an unusual degree. The faces are in miniature, in many cases portraits from life. They could be cut out and framed as portraits; each also is stamped with the individual passions of that terrible hour—hate, exultation, pain, courage, sorrow, despair. And yet with all this truth of detail the general spirit and effort

DEATH OF MONTGOMERY.—[JOHN TRUMBULL.]

of the scene is preserved. The onward movement, the rush, the onset of war, the harmony of lines, the massing of *chiaro-oscuro*, the brilliance and truth of color, are all there. One first gazes astonished at the skill of the artist, and ends by feeling his heart stirred and his emotions shaken as the leaves of the forest are blown by the winds of October, and his sympathies carried away by the grandeur and the terror of battle. Yes, when John Trumbull painted those two pictures, he was inspired by the fires of genius for once in his life. His later historical works are so inferior in all respects as scarcely to seem to be by the same hand.

Trumbull lived to see a taste for the arts growing up among his fellow-countrymen, and the awakening of the first feeble attempts to furnish art instruction in his native land to the artists of the future. He was President of the Academy of Fine Arts, of which he was one of the founders.

In the same year with Trumbull was born the greatest colorist and portrait-painter we have seen on this side of the Atlantic, Gilbert Stuart. The town of Narragansett, in the little State of Rhode Island, was the birthplace of this painter, who came of Scotch and Welsh descent, an alliance of blood whose individual traits were well illustrated in the life and character of the painter.

Fortune was becoming a little kinder to our artists. Stuart's dawning genius was directed at Newport by Cosmo Alexander, a Scotch portrait-painter of some merit, who took his pupil to Scotland and placed him in charge of Sir George Chambers. After various vicissitudes, comprising, as with so many of our early painters, an art apprenticeship in the studio of West, the young American artist settled for awhile abroad, and acquired such repute that he rivalled Sir Joshua Reynolds in the popular esteem: his brush was in demand by the first in the land; and the unfortunate Louis XVI. was included among his sitters. After this, in 1793, Stuart returned to America, painted the portraits of the leading citizens in our chief cities, and finally settled in Boston. The most important works he executed in this country were his well-known portraits of Washington, including the famous full-length painting, which represents the great man, not in the prime of his active days, as represented by Peale and Trumbull, but when, crowned with glory and honor in the majesty of a serene old age, he was approaching the sunset of life.

The character of Stuart was one of marked peculiarities, and offers points of interest scarcely equalled by that of any other American artist. The canny shrewdness and penetrating perception of the Scotchman was mellowed almost to the point of inconsistency by the warm and supple traits of his Welsh ancestry. An admirable story-teller himself, he in turn gave rise, by his oddities, to many racy anecdotes, some of which have been treasured up and well told by Dunlap, who, although inferior as a painter, deserves to be cordially remembered for his discursive but valuable book on early American painting.

As regards the art of Stuart, it can be safely affirmed that America has produced no painter who has been more unmistakably entitled to rank among men of genius as distinguished from those of talent. We assume

GENERAL KNOX.—[GILBERT STUART.]

that the difference between the two is not one of degree, but of kind. In the intellectual progress of the world the first leads, the other follows. One may have great talents, and yet really not enrich the world with a single new idea. He simply assents to the accepted, and lends it the aid of his powers. But genius, not content with things as they are, either gives us new truths or old truths in a new form. The greatest minds— Cæsar, Shakspeare, Goethe, Franklin—present us with a just combination of genius and talent: they both create and organize. Now, one may have great or little genius, but so far as he tells us something worth knowing in his own way, it is genius as distinguished from talent.

And this is why we say that Stuart had genius. He followed no beaten track, he gave in his allegiance to no canons of the schools. His eagle eye pierced the secrets of nature according to no prescribed rules. Not satisfied with surfaces or accessories, he gave us character as well. Nor did he rest here. In the technical requirements of his art he stands original and alone. That seemingly hard, practical Scotch nature of his was yet attuned like a delicate chord to the melody of color. Few more than he have felt the subtle relation between sound and color—for he was also a musician. In the handling of pigments, again, he stands pre-eminent among the artists of his generation. Why is it that his colors are as brilliant, as pure, as forcible, as harmonious, to-day as when he laid them on the canvas nearly a century ago? If you carefully examine his pictures you shall see one cause of the result explained. He had such confidence in his powers, and such technical mastery, that he needed not to experiment with treacherous vehicles; and, rarely mixing tints on the palette, laid pure blues, reds, or yellows directly on the canvas, and slightly dragged them together. Thus he was able to render the stippled, mottled semblance of color as it actually appears on the skin; to suggest, also, the prismatic effect which all objects have in nature; and, at the same time, by keeping the colors apart, to insure their permanence. Stuart generally painted thinly, on large-grained canvas, which gave the picture the softness of atmosphere. But sometimes, as in the case of the powerful portrait of General Knox, he loaded his colors. But even in that work he did not depart from his usual practice in rendering the flesh tints.

It has been alleged by some that Stuart was unable to do justice to the delicate beauty of woman, especially the refined type which is characteristic of the United States. He may have more often failed in this regard than in other efforts; but the force of the accusation disappears when one observes the extraordinary loveliness of such portraits as that of Mrs. Forrester, the sister of Judge Story, at Salem. But, indeed, it seemed to make little difference to him who the sitter happened to be. He entered into the nature of the individual, grasped the salient traits of his character, and, whether it was a seaman or a statesman, a triumphant general or a reigning belle, his unerring eye and his matchless brush rendered justice to them all.

Gilbert Stuart Newton, the nephew of Stuart, is a painter well known in England, where he early established himself; and, having been born at Halifax, and always remained a British subject, he more properly belongs to foreign art. But his education was gained in the studio of his uncle in Boston, and his style shows unmistakable traces of the teacher's methods. Newton executed some good portraits before abandoning his native land, including one of John Adams, which is in the Massachusetts Historical Society. He is known abroad chiefly as a *genre* painter of semi-literary compositions.

James Frothingham was also a pupil, and in some degree an imitator, of Stuart, who possessed unusual ability in portraiture, but it was confined to the painting of the head. Whether from the lack of early advantages —which was so remarkable that he had not even seen a palette when, self-

"BEGGAR'S OPERA."—[G. STUART NEWTON.]

taught, he was able to execute a very tolerable likeness — or because of natural limitation of power, Frothingham's talent seemed to stop with the neck of the sitter. The face would perhaps be reproduced with a force, a beauty of color, and a truth of character that oftentimes suggested the art of Stuart; while the hands or shoulders were almost ludicrously out of drawing and proportion.

Besides Frothingham, there were a number of American painters of celebrity, contemporaries of Stuart, but of unequal merit. Colonel Sargent acquired a repute in his time which it is difficult to understand at present. He seems to have been more of an amateur than a professional

"BABES IN THE WOOD."—[REMBRANDT PEALE.]

artist. His ablest work is the "Landing of the Pilgrims," of which a copy is preserved at Plymouth. Rembrandt Peale obtained a permanent reputation for his very able and truthful portrait of Washington. He bestowed upon it the best efforts of his mature years, and it received the compliment of being purchased by Congress for $2000—a large sum for an American painting in those days, when the purchasing power of money was greater than it is now. His "Court of Death" is a vast composition, that must candidly be considered more ambitious than successful. In such works as the "Babes in the Wood," Peale seems to foreshadow the *genre* art which has been so long coming to us. John Wesley Jarvis, a native of England, also enjoyed at one time much popularity as a portrait-painter. He was possessed of great versatility; was eccentric; a *bon vivant*, and excelled at telling a story. It is melancholy to record that, after many vicissitudes, he ended his days in poverty.

Thomas Sully was also a native of England, who came to this country in childhood, and lived to such a great age that it is difficult to realize that he was the contemporary of Trumbull and Stuart. Sully had great refinement of feeling, and reminds us sometimes of Sir Thomas Lawrence. This is shown in a certain favorite ideal head of a maiden which he reproduced in various compositions. One often recognizes it in his works. His portraits are also pleasing; but in the treatment of a masculine likeness the feebleness of his style and its lack of originality or strength are too often apparent. John Naegle, of Philadelphia, was a pupil of Sully, but first began his art career as apprentice to a coach-painter. Like many of our artists of that time, he tried his hand at a portrait of Washington; but he

FANNY KEMBLE.—[THOMAS SULLY.]

will be longest and best remembered by his vivid and characteristic painting of Patrick Lyon, the blacksmith, at his forge. This picture now hangs in the elegant gallery of the Philadelphia Academy of Fine Arts, where several of the masterpieces of our early painters may be seen hanging in company with it, among them West's "Christ Rejected," Vanderlyn's "Ariadne," and Allston's "Dead Man Restored to Life."

Born the year of the Declaration of Independence, John Vanderlyn, like most of the leading artists of this period of whom we are writing, lived to old age. His days were filled with hardships and vicissitudes:

and, unless he has since become aware of the fame he left behind, he was one of many to whom life has been a very questionable boon.

Vanderlyn was a farmer's boy on the Hudson River. It was one of those curious incidents by which Destiny sometimes makes us think there

ARIADNE.—[JOHN VANDERLYN.]

may be, after all, something more than blind action in her ways, that Aaron Burr, passing by his father's house, saw some rude sketches of the rustic lad with that keen eye of his. Burr discerned in them signs of promise, and invited him to come to New York. When Vanderlyn arrived Burr treated him kindly. Eventually the painter made a portrait of Theodosia, the beautiful and ill-fated daughter of his benefactor; and when Burr was under a cloud and found himself destitute in Europe, it was Vanderlyn who received and gave him shelter.

Much of the art-life of this painter was passed at Rome and in Paris. His varied fortunes, and the constant adversity that baffled him at every step, obliged him to resort to many a pitiful shift to keep soul and body together. It is owing to this cause that he so rarely found opportunity to do justice to the undoubted ability he possessed.

But Vanderlyn left at least two important creations, marked by genuine artistic feeling and beauty, that will long entitle him to a favorable position among American painters. "Marius Among the Ruins of Carthage" I have never seen, and can only speak of it by report; but that it is a work deserving to rank high in the art of the time seems to be proven not only by the applause it received at Rome, but also by the fact that it carried off the gold medal at the Salon in Paris. Such is the irony of fate that the artist was twice forced to pawn this medal. The second time he was unable to redeem it.

The "Ariadne" has unfortunately begun to show signs of age, and the browns into which the flesh tints are painted are commencing to discolor the delicate grays. An oil-painting, if properly executed, should hold its qualities for a longer time; but unhappily the works of too many good artists are affected in the same way. The "Ariadne" is, however, a noble composition, quite in classic style; and if not strikingly original, is a most creditable work for the early art of a young people.

Newport, Rhode Island's charming little city by the sea, once a thriving commercial centre, but now a favorite resort of culture and gayety and wealth, but always opulent in delightful Colonial and Revolutionary associations, and doubly attractive for the artistic memories that cling to it, and the treasures of our art which it contains—this was the birthplace of Edward G. Malbone, who, after a successful art-life in his native town and at Charleston, died at Newport, in 1807, at the early age of thirty-two. Miniature-painting was a favorite pursuit of our early artists. Some of our best portraits have been done by that means; but among all who have followed it in the United States none have excelled Malbone. although some, like John Fraser, of South Carolina, have been very clever at it. He succeeded in giving character to his faces to a degree unusual in miniature; while the coloring was rendered at once with remarkable delicacy, purity, and fidelity. His best works are probably the likeness of Ray Green, and the exquisitely beautiful group called the "Hours," which is carefully preserved in the Athenæum at Providence.

With the general public the name of no American artist of that time is probably more widely known than that of Washington Allston. He owes this in part, doubtless, to the fact that as a writer he also became identified with the literary circle at that time prominent in Eastern Massachusetts. He was born in 1779, at Waccamaw, South Carolina. Sent at

"THE HOURS."—[E. G. MALBONE.]   ORIGINAL SIZE.

seven years of age to Newport, both for health and instruction, he lived there ten years; and very likely associated with Malbone, and perhaps met Stuart there.

Subsequently Allston visited Italy, and then settled in London, where his talents received such ample recognition as to gain him the position of Academician. The mistake of his art-life—although it was perhaps advantageous to his fame at home—was probably his return to the United States while yet in his prime. The absence of influences encouraging to art growth, and of that sympathy and patronage so essential to a sensitive nature like that of Allston's, had a blighting effect on his faculties; and the many years he passed in Boston were years of aspiration rather than achievement. Allston has suffered from two causes. Overrated as an artist in his day, his reputation is now endangered from a tendency to award him less than justice. The latter may be due in part to the fact that Allston himself adopted a course of action that tended to repress rather than develop his art powers. In his desire to give intellectual and moral value and permanent dignity to his productions, and in his aversion to sensationalism in art, he treated his subjects with a deliberate severity which takes away from them all the feeling of spontaneity which is so delightful and important in works of the imagination. If his genius had been of the high order claimed by some, such a result would have been impossible. The emotional element would have sometimes asserted itself, and given to his finished works that warmth and attraction the lack of which, while they are intellectually interesting and worthy of great respect, prevents them from inspiring and winning our hearts, and has impaired the influence they might have had in advancing the progress of art in America.

That Allston might have produced paintings of more absolute power, seems evident from his numerous crayon sketches and studies for paintings, which are full of fire, energy, and beauty, delicate fancy, and creative power. One cannot wholly understand Allston's ability until he has seen those studies; and it cannot be too much regretted that he did not allow a freer rein to his brush when composing the works upon which he desired to establish his fame. When he did so far forget himself, we get a glimpse of the fervor and grandeur of the imagination that burned in that brain, whose thoughts were greater than its capacity for expression. It must also be granted that the works of Allston have the quality peculiar to the productions of original minds: it is not until they have been seen repeatedly that they reveal all that is in them. "Uriel in the Sun," "Jeremiah," and "The Dead Man Restored to Life," are probably the best of the finished works by which the solemn, mysterious, and impressive imagination of Allston can be best estimated. Without giving us new revelations regarding the secrets of color, as he was rather an imitator of the Venetian school than an originator, Allston can be justly considered one of the most agreeable colorists America has produced.

Few of those who recognize the late Samuel F. B. Morse as the inventor of our telegraphic system are aware that in early life he was an

"JEREMIAH."—[WASHINGTON ALLSTON.]

artist, and gave evidence of succeeding both in sculpture and painting. Although his preference was for the latter, we are inclined to think that he was best fitted to be a sculptor. He became the pupil of Allston in London, and modelled at that time a statue called the "Dying Hercules," which won the prize of a gold medal offered by the Adelphi Society of Arts for the best single figure. From that statue he afterward composed a painting of the same subject, which is now in New Haven, a work of unquestioned power, showing thorough anatomical knowledge and a crea-

"DYING HERCULES."—[SAMUEL F. B. MORSE.]

tive imagination. But, while there was reason to predict an interesting art career for the young American, circumstances beyond his control drifted him away from the chosen pursuit of his youth, and his fame and fortune were eventually achieved in the paths of science. It is interesting in this connection to read the words which Morse, suffering from the pangs of disappointment, wrote to one who asked his advice about becoming a painter: "My young friend, if you have determined to try the life of an artist, I wish you all success; but as you have asked my honest opinion, I must say that, if you can find employment in any other calling, I advise you to let painting alone. I have known so many young men—some of them of decided talent, too—who, after repeated trials and failures, became discouraged, gave up further effort, and went to ruin." Notwithstanding that such were his views when he abandoned art, did not Morse, in the prosperous hours of his life, sometimes look back to his early art with a pang of regret? But while he continued in the profession of art, his activity was such that the National Academy of Design owes its origin to him, and with him closed the first period of art in the United States.

We see that this division of our pictorial art—with the exception of Thomas Birch, of Philadelphia, a marine painter of some repute, and a few others of less note—was devoted to the figure; and, if sometimes feeble in result, was inspired by lofty motives. In historical art and portraiture it was, if not strictly original, yet often very able, and fairly maintained itself on a level with the contemporary art of Europe. Owing to the entire want of opportunities for professional education at home, our leading artists, with few exceptions, were forced to pass a good part of their lives in foreign studios.

We also find that a feeling for the beauty of form, as indicated in black and white, or in sculpture, was scarcely perceptible in this stage of our art. With the exception of Shem Drowne and Patience Wright, who modelled skilfully in wax, the sense for plastic art was altogether dormant in the country; while any progress in architecture, until in recent years, was hopelessly ignored. It is true that the active, restless intellect of Thomas Jefferson sought to endow the nation with a sixth order of architecture, called the Columbian, and patriotically resembling a stalk of Indian-corn. The small pillars made after this design are in one of the vestibules of the basement of the Capitol at Washington, where the ardent patriot may visit them, and see for himself the beginning and the end of the only order of architecture ever attempted in this country.

Through much tribulation, much earnest faith, and enthusiasm for art, our early painters prepared the way for the national art of the future. They met only moderate appreciation in their native land at that time. But we owe much to them; and in our preference for present methods—which must in turn be superseded by others—let us not forget the honor due to the pioneers of American art. In the first articulate utterances of a child, or in the dialect of an aboriginal tribe, lie the rudiments of a national tongue eventually carried to a high degree of culture; and the first rude art or poesy of a young people sometimes possesses touches of freshness, charming simplicity, or virile force which are too liable to be softened away beyond recall by the refinements of a later civilization.

II.

AMERICAN PAINTERS.

1828-1878.

THE generation immediately succeeding the American Revolution was devoted by the people of the young republic to adjusting its commercial and political relations at home and abroad. Early in this century, however, numerous signs of literary and art activity became apparent, and in 1815 the *North American Review* was founded. We mention this fact, although a literary event, as indicating the point in time when the nebulous character of the various intellectual influences and tendencies of the nation began to develop a certain cohesive and tangible form. It was about the same time that our art, subject to similar influences, began to assume a more definite individuality, and to exhibit rather less vagueness in its yearnings after national expression.

Gilbert Stuart, one of the most remarkable colorists of modern times, died in the year 1828. In the same year the National Academy of Design was founded. These two events, occurring at the same time, seem properly to mark the close of one period of our art history and the dawn of its successor; for notwithstanding the excellence of Stuart's art, and the virile character of the art of some of his contemporaries, yet their efforts had been spasmodic and unequal; much of it had been done abroad under foreign influences; and there was no sustained patronage or art organization at home which could combine their efforts toward a practical and common end. The first president of the new institution was Samuel F. B. Morse.

The National Academy of Design superseded a similar but less wisely organized society, which had led a precarious existence since 1801. With the new institution was collected the nucleus of a gallery of paintings and casts; and from the outset the idea suggested by its name was car-

"MUMBLE THE PEG."—[HENRY INMAN.]

ried out, by furnishing the most thorough opportunities for art-instruction the country could afford.

Although seemingly fortuitous, the establishment of the Academy of Design really marks the opening of a distinct era in the history of American art; during which it has developed into a rounded completeness to a degree that enables us, with some measure of fairness, to note the causes which led to it, which have nourished its growth, and which have made it a worthy forerunner of new methods for expressing the artistic yearnings of those who are to follow in years to come. It has indicated a notable advance in our art; it has, in spite of its weakness or imitation of foreign conventionalisms, possessed certain traits entirely and distinctively native; and has been distinguished by a number of artists of original and sometimes unusual ability, whose failure to accomplish all they sought was due rather to unfortunate circumstances than to the lack of genuine power, which in another age might have done itself more justice.

It is interesting to observe at this juncture that our art was influenced by exactly the same causes as our literature of the same period; and, like our national civilization, presents a singular reaching after original expression, modified sometimes by an unconscious imitation of foreign thought and methods.

There is one fact connected with the early growth of our art which is entirely contrary to the laws which have elsewhere governed the progress of art, and is undoubtedly due to the new and anomalous features of our social economy. Elsewhere the art-feeling has undeviatingly sought expression first in earthen-ware or plastic art, then in architecture and sculpture, and finally in painting. We have entirely reversed this order. The unsettled character of the population—especially at the time when emigration from the Eastern to the Western States caused a general movement from State to State—together with the abundance of lumber at that time, evidently offered no opportunity or demand for any but the rudest and most rapidly constructed buildings, and anything like architecture and decorative work was naturally relegated to a later period; and for the same reason, apparently, the art of sculpture showed little sign of demanding expression here until after the art of painting had already formulated itself into societies and clubs, and been represented by numerous artists of respectable abilities.

The art-feeling, which made itself apparent, vaguely and abortively, during our colonial period, began to demand freer and fuller expression soon after the new Republic had declared its independence; and, with scarce any patronage from the Government, assumed a degree of excellence surprising under the circumstances, and rarely reached by a nation in so short a time.

We recall no art of the past the order and conditions of whose growth resemble those of ours, except that of Holland after its wars of independence with Spain. The bane and the blessing of our art have been in the enormous variety of influences which have controlled its action. This has been a bane, because it has, until recently, prevented the concentration of effort which might lead to grand results and schools. It has been a blessing, because individual expression has thus found a vent, and mannerism has not yet become a conventional net, so thrown around our art as to prevent free action and growth. The American art of the last two generations has resembled the restless activity of a versatile youth, who seeks in various directions for the just medium by which to give direction to his life-work. If there has been, on the whole, a national bias in one direction more than another, it has been for landscape-painting.

Our intellectual state has also resembled the many-sided condition of Germany in the Middle Ages, waking up from the chaos of the Dark Ages, but broken up into different States, and representing different religions and races. But our position has been even more agitated and diverse; a general restlessness has characterized the community — a vast intellectual discontent with the present. Although strongly moved by pride of country, we have also been keenly sensitive to foreign influences, and have received impressions from them with the readiness of a photographic plate, although until recently the result has been assimilation rather than imitation; while internally we have been trying to harmonize race and sectional differences, which as yet are far from reaching homogeneity.

Together with all these individual influences must be included one of general application, to which nearly all our artists, of whatever race or section, have been subject in turn. In other countries the people have, by a long preparation, become ready to meet the artist half-way in appreciating and aiding him in his mission, either from the promptings of the religious sentiment to which his art has given ocular demonstration, or from a dominating and universal sense of beauty. With us it has been quite otherwise; for the artists have been in advance of public sentiment, and have had the misfortune to be forced to wait until the people could come up to them. In addition to the fact that in New England Puritan influences were at first opposed to art, the restless, surging, unequal, widely differing character of our people, brought face to face with the elementary problems of existence, founding new forms of government, and welding incongruous factors into one race and nation — in a word, wresting from fate our right to be — made us indifferent to the ideal, except in sporadic and individual cases, which indicated here and there that below the surface the poetic sentiment was preparing to assert itself; and that we, in turn, were preparing to acknowledge the great truth that art is an instinctive yearning of the race to place itself in accord with the harmony which rules the universe.

The result has been that a very large proportion of the artists of this period of our history have been compelled to endure far more than the traditionary hardships of the profession. They have been obliged to devote some of the best years of their lives to trade, and have not been able to take up art until late. To accuse American artists, as a class, of

PORTRAIT OF PARKE GODWIN.—[THOMAS LE CLEAR.]

being mercenary—a charge made quite too often—is really something akin to irony, so much more successful pecuniarily would the majority of them have been in mercantile pursuits. The heroism of our early painters, struggling, in obscure corners of the country, for opportunities to express their yearning after the ideal, without instruction, without art-influences, meeting little or no sympathy or encouragment, and in spite of these obstacles often achieving a respectable degree of excellence, is one of the most interesting, instructive, and sublime episodes in the history of art.

Growing out of this hesitating condition of our early art may be discerned a secondary cause, which occurred in so many cases as to be justly considered one of the forces which formed the careful, minute, painstaking style of much of our landscape art. We refer to the fact that many of the best of our early painters were first engravers on wood and steel. This gave them a minute, formal, and precise method of treatment, which led them to look at details rather than breadth of effect.

When we turn to the influences from abroad which stimulated American art during this period, we find that, while they fostered the growth of a certain æsthetic feeling, they at the same time instilled conventional methods and principles that deferred the development of a higher kind of art. It is greatly to be regretted that, notwithstanding the friendly relations between the United States and France, our art, when it was first looking to Europe for direction, should not have come in contact with that of France, which at that time, led by Gericault, Rousseau, Troyon, Delacroix, and other rising men, was becoming the greatest pictorial school since the Renaissance. But Italian art at that time was sunk to the lowest depths of conventionalism; while the good in the English art of the time was represented less by a school than by a few individuals of genius—Turner, Wilkie, Constable—who were so original that they failed to attract students whose first art ideas had been obtained in Italy.

The influence of Italy on our early art was shown by the tendency of our painters in that direction—as now they go to France and Germany—and this was due primarily to Allston and Vanderlyn. The latter, when at Rome, occupied the house of Salvator Rosa—apparently a trivial incident, but if we could trace all the influence it may have had on the fancy and tastes of the young American artist, we might find it was a powerful contributor to the formation of the early style of the landscape artists who followed him to Italy. This bias was also greatly assisted by the many paintings imported at that time from the Italian peninsula, which were either originals, bought cheaply during the disturbances which then convulsed Europe, or copies of more or less merit. These works made their way gradually over our country, from Boston to New Orleans; and, with the rapidly shifting fortunes of our families, have often been so completely placed out of sight and forgotten, that it is not an unfrequent instance for one to be unearthed in a remote country village, or farm-house that would never be suspected of harboring high art.

The larger portion of these foreign works came first to Boston, and

PORTRAIT OF FLETCHER HARPER

were hidden away somewhere in that vicinity, as in the case of the collection bequeathed to Bowdoin College by its founder; whose best specimens were eventually sold and scattered for a mere song by a faculty who were ignorant of their value, and thought they might at the same time aid morality and add an honest penny to the funds of the institution by selling its precious nudities, and thus remove them from the student's eye. As Allston and Stuart, who were colorists, also settled in Boston, after years of foreign study, these two circumstances contributed to make the Boston school from the first one of color—a fact less pronounced in the early art of New York.

It is to West and Allston and Trumbull that we are to attribute the English element in our arts. The prominent position they then occupied before the American public made their example and opinions of great importance with their countrymen, and undoubtedly contributed to suggest one of the most characteristic traits of American art, that is, the tendency to make art a means for telling a story, which has always been a prominent feature of English art. May we not also trace to English literature the bias which unconsciously led our painters to turn their attention to landscape with a unanimity that has until recently made our pictorial art distinctively a school of landscape painting? Cowper, Byron, and Wordsworth introduced landscape into poetry, and undoubtedly impelled English art in the same direction; and it was exactly at that time that our own poet, Bryant, undoubtedly influenced at the turning-point of his character by Wordsworth's solemn worship of nature, was becoming the pioneer of American descriptive poetry; while Irving was introducing the picturesque into our literature; and Cooper, with his vivid descriptions of our forests, was, like Irving, creating a whole class of subjects that were to be illustrated by the American artists of this period.

The influences cited as giving direction to the struggling efforts of art in our country during the early part of this century are illustrated with especial force by five portrait, figure, and landscape-painters, who may almost be considered the founders of this period of our art—Harding, Weir, Cole, Doughty, and Durand.

Chester Harding was a farmer's son, who, after an apprenticeship in agriculture, took up the trade of chair-maker at twenty-one, the time when the young Parisian artist has already won his *Prix de Rome*. After this he tried various other projects, including those of peddling and the keeping of a tavern; and then took his wife and child and floated on a flatboat down the Alleghany to Pittsburgh—at that time a mere settlement—in search of something by which to earn a bare living. There he took to sign-painting; and it was not until his twenty-sixth year that the idea of becoming a professional artist entered his head. An itinerant portrait-painter coming to the place first suggested the idea to Harding, who engaged him to paint the portrait of Mrs. Harding, and took his first art-

AN IDEAL HEAD.—[G. A. BAKER.]

lesson while looking over the artist's shoulder; and his first crude attempts so fascinated him that he at once adopted art as a profession, and in six months painted one hundred likenesses, such as they were, at twenty-five dollars each, and then settled in Boston, where he seems to have been taken up with characteristic enthusiasm. On going to England, Harding, notwithstanding the few advantages he had enjoyed, seemed to compare so favorably with portrait-painters there that he was patronized by the first noblemen of the land. Although belonging also to the latter part of the period immediately preceding that now under consideration, yet Harding was, on the whole, an important factor in the art which dates from the founding of the National Academy, and was one of the strongest of the group of portrait-painters naturally associated with him, such as Alexander, Waldo, Jarvis, and Ingham. There was something grand in the personality of Harding, not only in his almost gigantic physique but also his sturdy, frank, good-natured, but earnest and indomitable character, which causes him to loom up across the intervening years as a type of the people that have felled forests, reclaimed waste places, and given thews and sinews to the Republic that in a brief century has placed itself in the front rank of nations.

While Harding, with all his artistic inequalities, fairly represented the portrait art of Boston at that period, Henry Inman may be considered as holding a similar position in New York. As a resident of that city and a pupil of Jarvis, he enjoyed advantages of early training superior to those of most of our painters of that day. Exceedingly versatile, and excelling in miniature, and doing fairly well in *genre* and landscape, Inman will be best known in future years by his admirable oil portraits of some of the leading characters of the time. He was a man of great strength and symmetry of character, who would have won distinction in any field, and his early death was a misfortune to the country.

New York became the centre for a number of excellent and characteristic portrait-painters soon after Inman established his reputation—such as Charles Loring Elliott, Baker, Hicks, Le Clear, Huntington, and Page, the contemporaries of Healy, Ames, Hunt, and Staigg, of Boston, and Sully, of Philadelphia—all artists of individual styles and characteristic traits of their own. Sully, owing to his great age, really belonged also to the preceding period of our art.

In Elliott we probably find the most important portrait-painter of this period of American art. It was a peculiarity of his intellectual growth that only by degrees did he arrive at the point of being able to seize a simple likeness. But it is not at all uncommon for genius to falter in its first attempts; and Elliott was one of the few artists we have produced who could be justly ranked among men of genius, as distinguished from those of talents, however marked. Stuart excelled all our portrait-painters in purity and freshness of color and masterly control of pigments; but he

"THE JUDGMENT OF PARIS."—[HENRY PETERS GREY.]

was scarcely more vigorous than Elliott in the wondrous faculty of grasping character. Herein lay this artist's strength. He read the heart of the man he portrayed, and gave us not merely a faithful likeness of his outward features, but an epitome of his intellectual life and traits, almost clutching and bringing to light his most secret thoughts. In studying the portraits of Elliott we learn to analyze and to discern the essential and irreconcilable difference between photography and the highest order of painting. The sun is a great magician, but he cannot reproduce more than lies on the surface—he cannot suggest the soul. He is like a truthful but unwilling witness, who gives only part, and not always the best part, of the truth. But then the genius of the great artist steps in, completes the testimony, and presents before us suggestions of the immortal being that shall survive when the mortal frame and the sun which photographs it have alike passed away.

Baker, on the other hand, has excelled in rendering the delicate color and loveliness of childhood, and the splendor of the finest types of American feminine beauty. The miniatures of Staigg are also among the most winning works of the sort produced by our art. Among other excellent miniature-painters of this period was Miss Goodrich, of whose personal history less is known than of any other American artist.

William Page occupies a phenomenal position in the art of this period, because, unlike most of our painters, he has not been content to take art methods and materials as he found them, but has been an experimentalist and a theorist as well, and therefore belongs properly to more recent phases of our art. Thus, while he has achieved some singularly successful works in portraiture and historical painting, he has done much that has aroused respect rather than enthusiasm.

If less refined in aim and treatment than Page in his rendering of female beauty, Henry Peters Grey, who was also an earnest student of Italian Renaissance art, succeeded sometimes to a degree which, if far below that of the masters whom he studied, was yet in advance of most of such art as has been executed by American painters, at least until very recently. "The Judgment of Paris" is certainly a clever if not wholly original work, and the figure of Venus a fine piece of form and color.

Daniel Huntington, the third president of the National Academy of Design, is a native of New York city, and has enjoyed advantages and successes experienced by very few of our early artists. A pupil of Morse and Inman, he is better known by the men of this generation as a pleasing portrait-painter; but the most important of his early efforts were in what might be called a semi-literary style in *genre* and historical and allegorical or religious art, in which departments he has won a permanent place in our annals by such compositions as "Mercy's Dream," "The Sibyl," and "Queen Mary Signing the Death-warrant of Lady Jane Grey."

While portraiture has been the field to which most of our leading painters of the figure have directed their attention during this period, *genre* has been represented by several artists of decided ability, who, under more favorable art auspices, might have achieved superior results. Inman was one of the first of our artists to make satisfactory attempts in *genre*. If circumstances had allowed him to devote himself entirely to any one of the three branches he pursued, he might have reached a higher position than he did. But the most important *genre* artist of the early part of this period was William Sidney Mount, the son of a farmer on Long Island. Associated first with his brother as a sign-painter, he eventually, in 1828, took up *genre* painting. Mount lacked ambition, as he himself confessed; he was too easily influenced by the rapidly won approval of the public to cease improving his style, and early returned to his farm on Long Island. Mount was not remarkable as a colorist, although it is quite possible he might have succeeded as such with superior advantages; but he was in other respects a man of genius, who as such has not been surpassed by the numerous *genre* artists whom he preceded, and to whom he showed by his example the resources which our native domestic life can furnish to the *genre* painter. This American Wilkie had a keen eye for the humorous traits of our rustic life, and rendered them with an effect that sometimes suggests the old Dutch masters. "The Long Story" and "Bargaining for a Horse" are full of inimitable touches of humor and shrewd observations of human nature. F. W. Edmonds, who was a contemporary of Mount, although a bank cashier, found time from his business to produce many clever *genre* paintings, showing a keener eye for color, but less snap in the drawing and composition, than Mount.

In other departments of the figure at this period of our art, Robert W. Weir holds a prominent position as one of our pioneers in the distinctive branch called historical painting. Of Huguenot descent, and gaining his artistic training in Italy, after severe struggles at home, his career illustrates several of the influences which have been most apparent in forming American art. Although not a servile imitator of foreign and classic art, and showing independence of thought in his practice and choice of subjects, Weir's style is pleasing rather than vigorous and original. It shows care and loving patience, as of one who appreciates the dignity of his profession, but no marked imaginative force, nor does he introduce or suggest any new truths. Such a massive composition, however, as the "Sailing of

"MIRANDA."—[DANIEL HUNTINGTON.]

the Pilgrims," while it scarcely arouses enthusiasm, causes us to wonder that we should so early have produced an art as conscientious and clever as this. The portrait of Red Jacket, and the elaborate painting called "Taking the Veil," are also works of decided merit. Enjoying a serene old age, this revered painter yet survives, still wielding his brush, and annually exhibiting creditable pictures in the Academy.

"A SURPRISE."—[WILLIAM SIDNEY MOUNT.]

In the works of the figure-painters we have spoken of there is evident an earnest pursuit of art, attended sometimes with very respectable results; but, with the exception of here and there a portrait-painter of real genius, we do not discover in their paintings much that is of value in the history of art, except as indicating the existence of genuine æsthetic feeling in the country demanding expression in however hesitating and abortive a manner. But when we come to the subject of landscape-painting, we enter upon a field in which originality of style is apparent, and a certain consistency and harmony of effort. Minds of large reserve power meet us at the outset, moved by strong and earnest convictions, and often expressing their thoughts in methods entirely their own. Thoroughly, almost fanatically, national by nature, even when their art shows traces of foreign influence, and drawing their subjects from their native soil, they have created an art which can fairly claim to be ranked as a school, whatever be the position assigned to it in future ages. English, French, Irish, African, and Spaniard have alike vied in painting the scenery of this beautiful country, and mingling their fame and identifying their lives with " its hills, rock-ribbed and ancient as the sun," its mountain streams and meadow lands, its primeval forests, and the waves that break upon its granite shores.

It is to three artists of great natural ability that the origin of American landscape-painting can be traced—Cole, Doughty, and Durand. Although the youngest of the three, the first seems to have antedated Doughty by a few months in adopting this branch of art professionally; while Durand, older than Cole by several years, yet did not take up landscape-painting until some years after him.

Thomas Cole died in the prime of life, at the age of forty-seven, but there are few characters in the history of the country that have made a deeper impression. Singularly versatile, inspired by a powerful imagination, possessing a pure and lofty character, and animated by the noblest of sentiments, we feel before his greatest works—through all the imperfections of his art, through all the faltering methods with which his genius sought to express itself—that a vast mind here sought feebly to utter great thoughts (which he has doubtless already learned to utter with more truth in another world); we see that unmistakable sign of all minds of a high order, the evidence that the man was greater than his works. It is not dexterity, technique, knowledge, that impresses us in studying the works of Cole, so much as character. One feels that in them is seen the handwriting of one of the greatest men who have ever trod this continent.

Thomas Cole, the first artist who ever painted landscape professionally in America—unless we except the few faltering landscape-paintings of John Frazer, the miniature artist of the previous century—was born in England, but he was of American ancestry, and his parents returned to this country in his childhood. The difficulties with which he had to contend at the outset of his art career form an affecting picture. From infancy he had been fond of the pencil; and the tinting of wall-paper in his father's factory at Steubenville, Ohio, gave him a slight practice in the harmony of colors. In the mean time he took up engraving, but was

"TAKING THE VEIL."—[ROBERT WEIR.]

diverted from this pursuit by a travelling German portrait-painter, who gave him a few lessons in the use of oil-colors. He began with portraiture, and resolved to be an artist, although the failure of his father's business brought the whole family on him for support. The struggles through which the youth now passed make a long and painful story. Through it all he retained his bias for art, and at twenty-two began to draw scenery, from nature, along the banks of the Monongahela. Dunlap has well said, "To me the struggles of a virtuous man endeavoring to buffet fortune, steeped to the very lips in poverty, yet never despairing, or a moment ceasing his exertions, is one of the most sublime objects of contemplation."

After several years of this severe hardship, Cole finally drifted to New York, and eventually attracted notice. When the National Academy of Design was founded in 1828, Cole and Doughty were simultaneously winning success, and giving a permanent character to the art which for half a century was destined to be most prominent on the walls of the Academy.

So far as foreign technical influences can be traced in the compositions of Cole, they are those of Claude and Salvator Rosa. He revisited England at the time when Turner and Constable were establishing their fame, and producing such an influence on the great school of French landscape art which has since succeeded. It is interesting to think what would have been the character of our landscape art if Cole had been favorably impressed by the broad and vigorous style of these painters. But he does not seem to have been ripe for the audacious and sometimes more truthful methods of modern landscape, and expressed himself with warmth regarding what he considered the extravagances of Turner.

The art of Cole was however, largely biassed by the literature of England. The influence of both Bunyan and Walter Scott can be traced in his works; while the serious turn of his mind gave a solemn majesty and a religious fervor to his compositions, which command our deep respect, even when we fail altogether to concede complete success to his artistic efforts. For this reason Cole has wielded, more than most of our artists, a powerful influence outside of his art with a people which, with all its volatility, yet maintains the traditions of a deeply religious ancestry. It was in this many-sidedness of his genius, that brought him into contact with widely varied sympathies, that Cole's chief power consisted; for if we look at his work from the art point of view alone, we are impressed with its inequality, the lack of early art influences which it exhibits, and an attempt sometimes at dramatic force which occasionally lapses into mere sensationalism. But in all his compositions there are evident a rapturous love of nature, and the energy and yearning of a mind seeking to find expression for a vast ideal. Cole was what very few of our artists have been—an idealist. The work by which he will be longest and best remembered in the art of his country is the noble series called the "Course of Empire," consisting of five paintings, representing a nation's rise, progress, decline, and fall, and the change which comes over the abandoned scenery as the once superb capital returns to the wildness and solitude of nature. The last of the series, entitled "Desolation"—a gray silent waste, haunted by the bittern, with here and there a crumbling column reflected in the deserted harbor, where gleaming fleets once floated, and imperial pageants were seen in the pavilions along the marble piers—is one of the most remarkable productions of American art. But with all the enthusiasm which Cole aroused among his contemporaries, his influence seems to have

"DESOLATION."—[FROM "THE COURSE OF EMPIRE," BY THOMAS COLE.]

been to give dignity to landscape art rather than to impress his thoughts and methods on other artists. It is true that he seized the characteristics of our scenery with a truth which came not only from close study, but also from deep affection for the land whose mountains and lakes he painted, and thus led our first landscapists to observe the great variety and beauty of their own country. But, on the other hand, a certain hardness in his technique probably rendered him less influential as a leader than Doughty and Durand. The former, if inferior in general capacity to Cole, was more emphatically the artist by nature.

Thomas Doughty was in the leather business until his twenty-eighth year, when, without any previous training, he threw up the trade, and adopted the profession of landscape-painter. There is an audacity, a self-confidence, in the way our early painters entered on the art career, without instruction in the theory and practice of their art, which is charming for the simplicity it shows, but would tend to bring the efforts of these artists into contempt if the results had not often justified their audacity, for they were sometimes men of remarkable ability. There have been many greater landscape-painters than Doughty, but few who have done so well with such meagre opportunities for instruction. He seems, also, to have been successful in attracting favorable notice in England as well as here, although at a time when English landscape art was at its zenith. The soft, poetic traits, the tender, silvery tones, that distinguished Doughty's style, were entirely original with him, and have undoubtedly had much influence in forming the style of some of the landscapists who succeeded him.

In Asher B. Durand, a Huguenot by descent, and the only one of the three founders of American landscape-painting who survives to our time to enjoy a green old age, we find a nature as strong as that of Cole. The equal of that artist in the sum of his intellectual powers, we discover in him a different quality of mind. Similar as they are in high moral purpose and a profound reverence for the Creator, as represented in his works, Cole was the most imaginative and inspirational of the two, stirred more by the fire of genius; while Durand, with a more equable temperament and a larger experience, produced results that are more satisfactory from an art point of view.

Few artists have shown greater capacity than Durand in successfully following entirely distinct branches of art. As a steel-engraver, who in this century has produced work that is much superior to his superb engraving of Vanderlyn's "Ariadne?" Who of our artists has been able both to design and to engrave such a work as his "Musidora?" After employing the burin so admirably, he took up portrait-painting, and by such portraits as his head of Bryant placed himself by the side of our leading portrait-painters. Still unsatisfied with the success won thus far, Durand, in his thirty-eighth year, directed his efforts to landscape-painting, and at once became not only a pioneer but a master in this department. The care he had been obliged to give to engraving was undoubtedly of great assistance to him in enabling him to render the lines of a composition with truth; while his practice of studying character in portraiture gave him insight into the individuality of trees—he invested them with a humanity like that which the ancient Greeks gave to their forests when

A STUDY FROM NATURE.—[A. B. DURAND.]

they made them the haunt of the dryads. It is to this that we doubtless owe the massive handling, the fresh and vigorous treatment of trees in such solemn and majestic landscapes as " The Edge of the Forest," in the Corcoran Gallery at Washington. The art of Durand is wholly national; few of our painters owe less to foreign inspiration. Here he learned the various arts that gave him a triple fame, here he found the subjects for his compositions, and his name is destined to endure as long as American art shall endure.

Among the most prominent of the landscape-painters who succeeded the founders of the art among us, and were, like them, inspired by a rev-

"NOON BY THE SEA-SHORE."—BEVERLY BEACH.—[J. F. KENSETT.]

erent spirit and lofty poetic impulses, John F. Kensett holds a commanding position. Like Durand, he began his career with the burin, and after working for the American Bank-note Company, drifted into painting. Circumstances seem to have favored him beyond many of his compeers, and he was early permitted to visit England and the Continent, and spent seven years abroad. Notwithstanding so long an association with foreign schools, especially the Italian, we find very little evidence of foreign art in the style of Kensett. He was fully as original as Durand, and saw and represented nature in his own language. His methods of rendering a bit of landscape were tender and harmonious, and entirely free from any attempt at sensationalism. So marked was the latter characteristic especially, that before the great modern question of the values began to arouse much attention in the ateliers of Paris, Kensett had already grasped the perception of a theory of art practice which has since become so prominent in foreign art; although, naturally, it is not in all his canvases that this attempt to interpret the true relations of objects in nature is equally evident. We see it brought out most prominently in some of his quiet, dreamy coast scenes, in which it is not so much things as feelings that he tries to render or suggest. In them also is most apparent an endeavor after breadth of effect, which is a sign of mastery when successfully carried out. Mr. Kensett's art consisted in a certain inimitably winning tenderness of tone — a subtle poetic suggestiveness. His small compositions, as a rule, are more satisfying than his larger pictures, in which the thinness of his technique is sometimes too prominent. The career of Kensett, who died but a few years ago, is one of the most complete and symmetrical in our art history.

A contemporary of Kensett, but still surviving him, George L. Brown, of Boston, struggled heroically and successfully with the early difficulties

"ALTORF, BIRTH-PLACE OF WILLIAM TELL."—[GEORGE L. BROWN.]

of his life; and, yielding to the seductive influences of Italian scenery, devoted his art to representing it, with results that entitle him to an honorable position. The effects he has sought are luminousness and color. Mr. Brown's method of using colors was formed, to a certain extent, on that of the Italian landscape art of the time; and, while often brilliant and poetic, reminds us sometimes of the studio rather than of the free, pure, magical opulence of the atmosphere and sunlight of the scenery he portrayed. It can be frankly conceded, however, that he has been no slavish copyist of a style; but while acknowledging the force of foreign influences, has yet given abundant evidence of a personality of his own; and in such works as his "Bay of New York," which is owned by the Prince of Wales, and some of his views among the liquid streets of Venice lined with mouldering palaces, and skimmed by gondolas darting hither and thither like swallows, he has shown himself to be a true poet and an admirable painter.

III.

AMERICAN PAINTERS.

1828-1878.

NO school of art ever came more rapidly into being than the landscape school which owes its rise to Cole, Doughty, and Durand. Up to this time portraiture had been the field in which American painters had achieved their most signal successes. But now the majority of our artists of ability turned their attention to the representation of scenery; and for forty years a long list of painters have made the public familiar with their native land, and have thus, at the same time, stimulated a popular interest in art.

It is impossible to mention here more than a few of those who, as landscape-painters, have won a local or national reputation among us. Nor is it essential, while recognizing the great importance and undoubted merit of our landscape art, to exaggerate its relative value and position. While it has, in most cases, been the result of a true artistic feeling and a genuine, if not very demonstrative, enthusiasm for nature on the part of the artists who have devoted their lives to its pursuit, and while it has given us much that is pleasing, much that is improving, much that is poetic, and occasionally some examples of a high order of landscape-painting—yet, as a whole, our school of landscape seems scarcely to be entitled to the highest rank. The wonder is that it has been of such average excellence, for the environing conditions have apparently not been favorable. The influences among which it sprung have been so often prosaic or uninspiring, that, notwithstanding its fertility, we find the result to lean to quantity rather than quality. The ideal and emotional elements in art have not been sufficiently dominant; while the topographical and the mechanical notions regarding the end of landscape art have prevailed.

Until recently this school has contented itself with the superficial as-

"BROOK IN THE WOODS."—[WORTHINGTON WHITTREDGE.]

pect of nature rather than with the subtle suggestions by which it appeals to the soul. An absence of imaginative power has been too apparent, and a lack of the energy and earnestness born of large natures and absorbing enthusiasm; and the abundant variety or individuality of style, while indicating self-reliant, independent action, sometimes has also been a result of the want of solid training, or failure to grasp the accepted principles which underlie art practice. There has been a general average of native ability in the artists—a certain dead level of excellence in the quality of the works offered at our annual exhibitions—which was good as far as it went; but, except on rare occasions, it seldom arrested and enchained attention by the expression of daring technique or imaginative power, as the outcome of concerted influences exerted in one direction, and resulting in typical representative minds of vast resources, bounding into the arena and challenging the admiration of the world. Artists we have undoubtedly had occasionally, during this period, who have been endowed with genius to win renown; but they have, like Cole, either lacked the training and influences—the long succession of national heredity in art practice which are well-nigh indispensable to the highest success; or, like Church, yielding to the impulse of a prosaic environment, they have stopped short of the highest flights of art, and their imagination has been curbed to the subordinate pursuit of rendering the actual rather than the ideal.

In technique, also—if we may be permitted modestly to express an opinion on the subject—this school has seemed to be, on the whole, weak and vacillating, being impelled by no definite aim. It has dealt with detail rather than masses; it has concerned itself with parts rather than general effect. Thus, while the rendering of details has sometimes been given with great fidelity, the spirit of the scene has eluded the artist, and a work which dazzles us at first, fails, therefore, to hold the imagination of the observer, and becomes flat and insipid on repeated inspection. The reverse is the case with works of art of the first order.

We also find in the art of this school weakness in a knowledge of—or at least in the power of appreciating—the vast significance of the line in art. Too many American paintings, which have been clever in color, have been almost ruined by the palpable ignorance they display of the elements of drawing. Inability to compose effectively—or, in other words, to perceive the harmony which is the dominant idea of true art—has also been too frequent a characteristic of this school. While in the application

LANDSCAPE COMPOSITION.—[R. W. HUBBARD.]

of colors a lack of nerve has been exhibited which gives to many of these works an appearance of thinness, that becomes painfully apparent when they have been painted a few years. These observations apply no less to the figure-painting than the landscape art of this period of American art; and a general absence of warmth and earnestness is the impression which a survey of the field leaves upon the mind of the candid observer.

There is nothing in this to surprise or to discourage, if we frankly consider the surrounding circumstances. Great art is the child of repose;

the restlessness, the feverish activity of the country, eminently encouraging to some pursuits, is, if not fatal to the arts, at least opposed to their highest development; the vast multiplicity of aims agitating the people has thus far prevented that concentration of effort which meets with a response in the enthusiasm of artistic genius. Instead of being discouraged, therefore, by the quality of the art we have already produced, we accept it as strong evidence that the American people have a decided natural turn for the arts, which only awaits a more favorable condition of the nation to reach a higher plane of excellence.

Nor does the general absence of imaginative power in our art seem to us proof that we are by nature destined to remain a prosaic people. Aside from the fact that already years ago we had such imaginative artists as Hamilton, Lafarge, Vedder, and others, we consider that the wonderful inventive quality of the American mind toward scientific and mechanical discovery argues a highly creative imagination. Herbert Spencer it is who proves somewhere that imagination must enter into the working out of the problems of inventive science. Hitherto the nation's needs have stimulated the imagination in that direction; but under new conditions there is little reason to doubt that the same faculty will become subservient to the creation of an original and powerful school of art in America.

But while admitting the weak points of our landscape art, and that the highest flights of which landscape-painting is capable have not always been reached by our artists, we should be careful, on the other hand, lest we fail to award them the merit which is justly their due for persevering endeavor, and frequently for great natural ability. Let us, in justice, ungrudgingly allow the discriminating praise that some out of a large number are undoubtedly entitled to claim. If we mention them individually rather than by the classification of schools, it is simply because, for the reasons already stated, scarce any of our artists have founded schools; although we may, perhaps, without inconsistency, speak of the efforts of artists of altogether different styles, but treating the same class of subjects, as a school. It is in this sense that we allude to our school of landscape.

With certain important exceptions, to be noted in another chapter, the American art of this period has, on the whole, been concerned chiefly with the objective; and it could not have well been otherwise, for any other form of art at such a time would have utterly failed to carry the people with it, and thus missed of producing that gradual æsthetic education which is the province of a national art.

Not only for this reason has our school of landscape art vindicated its right to be, and established its claim on our respectful attention, but also because it has owed little to foreign influences—springing rather from environing circumstances, as naturally as the flowers of May follow the departure of winter.

And thus, as after a long winter a few warm spring days cover the orchard with an affluence of blossoms, so at this time from many quarters of the land artists appeared, especially in the field of landscape art; and

"THE VASTY DEEP."—[WILLIAM T. RICHARDS.]

one can hardly believe that where, but a few years before, the Indian and the buffalo and the wolf had roamed at their own wild will, artists now arose, armed with an ability to discern the beauties of their native land, to direct the prosaic thoughts of the pioneer to the loveliness of the nature which surrounded him, and to make for themselves an enduring name. Ohio, the Massachusetts of the West, for example, which became a State as late as 1800, was in the early part of this period especially prolific in artists, who, if they did not find instruction or a public on the spot, were at least enabled, with the increasing means of communication, to go to New York and Boston, or to wander over to the studios and art wealth of

Europe. In other lands and ages the poetic sentiment has first found a vent in lyrics and idyls; but with us the best poetry has been in the landscape-painting which was created by the sons of those whose ploughs first broke the soil of this continent with a Christian civilization. At this period, also, we note the advent of an influence which doubtless aided to promote a more rapid pursuit of the new art impulse of the nation. Steam, the mighty magician which drives the locomotive and the steamship, is in bad repute with the conservatives who are not in sympathy with the progressive movements of the age; and yet among all the other results of which it has been the wonderful agent, we must ascribe its patronage of art. It is undoubtedly to the far greater facilities for going from place to place, which followed the introduction of steam, that we must partly attribute the rapid success of many of the artists who appeared in our country at that time in such unexpected numbers.

It was in 1841 that Leutze went to Düsseldorf to study, and thus introduced a new influence into our art, which hitherto, so far as it had acknowledged foreign influences, had been swayed by the schools of Italy and Britain. The effect was evident when, a few years later, Worthington Whittredge, a native of Ohio, went to Düsseldorf, and studied under the guidance of Achenbach. Very naturally his style showed for a time the effect of foreign methods; but he was guided by a native independence of action that enabled him in the end to assimilate rather than to imitate, like most of our artists at this time, and his later landscapes are thoroughly individual and American, although doubtless improved by foreign discipline. As a faithful delineator of the various phases of American wood interiors, Mr. Whittredge has deservedly won a permanent place in the popular favor. Some of his landscapes, representing the scenery of the great West, have also been large in treatment and effective in composition; but his skies sometimes lack atmosphere and ideality.

Like his master, Durand, J. W. Casilear began his career as an engraver; and the success he achieved in this department is attested by his very clever engraving of Huntington's "Sibyl." Since he drifted into landscape-painting, Casilear has produced many delicately finished and poetic scenes, distinguished by elegance and refinement rather than dash or originality; and somewhat the same observations would apply to the tender landscapes of James A. Suydam. In such dreamy, pleasant, but not very vigorous paintings as that of his "Valley of the Pemigewasset," Samuel L. Gerry has also attracted favorable attention.

"HIGH TORN, ROCKLAND LAKE."—[JASPER F. CROPSEY.]

The work of a genuine poet is apparent in the canvases of R. W. Hubbard. Repose and pensive harmoniousness of treatment characterize his simple and winsome, if not stirring, transcripts of the more familiar phases of our scenery. They are idyls in color. What Hubbard has done for New England landscape, J. R. Meeker, of St. Louis, has attempted for the "lakes of the Atchafalaya, fragrant and thickly embowered with blossoming hedges of roses," and the live-oaks spreading their vast arms, like groined arches of Gothic cathedrals, festooned with the mystically trailing folds of the Spanish moss, along the lagoons of the South-west, where the sequestered shores are haunted by the pelican and the gayly colored crane, and the groves are melodious with the rapturous lyrics of the mockingbird, the improvisatore of the woods. If not always successful in the tone of his pictures, it may be conceded that Mr. Meeker has approached his subject with a reverent and poetic spirit, and has often rendered these scenes with much feeling and truth.

Still another aspect of our scenery has been reproduced with fidelity by W. T. Richards, of Philadelphia. We refer to the long reaches of silvery shore and the sand-dunes which are characteristic of many parts of our Atlantic coast. He has often painted woodland scenes with great patience, but, as it seems to us, with too much detail, and with greens which are open to a charge of being crude and violent. But in his beach effects Mr. Richards maintains an important position; and if slightly mannered, has yet developed a style of subject and treatment which very effectively represents certain distinguishing features of our solemn coasts. Some of his water-color paintings have scarcely been surpassed, as, for example, the noble representations of the bleak, snow-like, cedar-tufted dunes along the Jersey shore.

The extraordinary variety of the effects of American landscape is again shown by the gorgeousness of our autumnal foliage. It has been objected by some that it is too vivid for art purposes. We consider this a matter of individual taste. There is nothing more absurd in trying to render the effects of sunset, or the scarlet and gold of an American

"THE PARSONAGE."—[A. F. BELLOWS.]

forest in the dreamy days of the Indian summer, than in undertaking to paint the splendor of many-colored drapery in an Oriental crowd, which is considered a legitimate subject for the artist who has a correct eye for color. It is not in the subject, but in the artist, that the difficulty lies. Some of our painters have seized these autumnal displays with fine feeling and excellent judgment. Kensett is an example; another is J. F. Cropsey, who, beginning life as an architect, became eventually an agreeable delineator of our autumnal scenery, and at one time executed a number of paintings remarkable for their truth and artistic beauty. His later work has scarcely sustained the early reputation he justly acquired. At its best, his style was crisp, strong in color, and sometimes very bold in composition. Mr. C. P. Cranch, who was associated with Cropsey in Italy, and who is well known as a writer, has exhibited in his Venetian landscapes a correct perception of color, while his method lacks firmness of drawing, and shows traces of foreign influence more than that of many of our artists who studied abroad at this time. R. H. Fuller, who was a night-watchman on the police force of Chelsea, Massachusetts, and died in 1871, was an artist whose educational opportunities were excessively meagre. But he had a fine eye for color and atmospheric effect, and some of his landscapes are painted with a full brush, and are tender and beautiful. F. D. Williams, before he left Boston for Paris, also developed a strong scheme of handling and color which was at once pleasing and original. F. H. Shapleigh has likewise shown an excellent feeling for some of nature's more quiet effects, and his coast scenes are attractive, although lacking somewhat in force.

As one considers this field of American art, he is increasingly astonished to find how strikingly it exemplifies one of the leading traits of a national school in the entire originality and individuality with which each of our prominent landscapists of this period interprets nature, even when he has studied more or less in Europe. Whatever may be the general defect of refinement rather than strength, and other weaknesses characteristic of our school of landscape art, it must be admitted that its representative artists have been often sturdily independent, and that their merits as well as their defects are entirely their own. What difference there is between the carefully finished but rich, massive foliage of David Johnson, suggesting the strength of the old English masters of landscape, and the dreamy, mellow pastoral meadow lands, wooded slopes, and dimpling lakes of our Green Mountains, veiled by a luminous haze and steeped in repose, which are so delicately portrayed by the brush of J. B. Bristol! Few of the landscape-painters of this school have produced more agreea-

LANDSCAPE WITH CATTLE.—[JAMES HART.]

ble results with their brush. What points of divergence there are, again, between the landscapes of W. L. Sonntag and A. F. Bellows!—the one adopting a scheme of tone and color apparently out of the focus of nature, yet so using it in rendering ideal compositions as to achieve results which place him by the side of our leading poets of nature. To him landscape-painting seems to be not so much a means to give faithful transcripts of actual scenes as to represent the ideals of his fancy; and as such we accept them with thankfulness, for they not only serve to give us pleasure, but also to illustrate the many-sided phases of art. Bellows, on the other hand, both in oil and *aquarelle*, has attempted minute reproductions of nature; and, while sometimes suggesting the impression of labor rather more than is consistent with breadth of effect, has faithfully and charmingly interpreted the idyllic side of our rural life. If he had not been a poet in color, we might have expected of him pastoral lyrics imbued with the spirit of Cowper or Thompson. Early study at the school of Antwerp, and the pursuit of *genre* for some years, have enabled Mr. Bellows skilfully to diversify his attractive village pictures and representations of our noble New England elms with groups of figures. He is justly entitled to be called the American Birket Foster.

It is instructive, in this connection, to observe the first landscapes of George Inness, which properly belong in style to the early and distinctively American school of landscape, while his recent method has identified him with the later graduates of the ateliers of Paris. Samuel Colman is another landscape-painter whose art is identified both with this school and with that of the period on which we are now entering. Educated here, and influenced by a fine eye for color, foreign travel has broadened his sympathies, modified his technique, and led him to look with favor upon later methods.

The landscapes of William and James Hart represent still another phase of our art. Both began life as apprentices to a coach-painter, but gradually identified themselves with the great throng of all ages who have become the votaries of nature. There is cleverness and dexterity in their work, a fine perception of the external beauty of the slopes and vales and woods of our land, and brilliant color; but it is sometimes marred by hardness of handling, and lack of juiciness or warmth of feeling; in other words, it is too exclusively objective, as if only the physical and not also the mental eye had been concerned in the painting of their works. James Hart has of late years added cattle to his landscapes with excellent success, and holds a prominent position among the very few respectable painters of animal life whom the American art of this period can justly claim.

Mr. Horace Robbins, successful in seizing certain aspects of mountain scenery, with a fine feeling for atmospheric grays, and Mr. Arthur Parton, who very pleasingly renders trees, and some of the sober effects of our dim November days, although among our younger painters, justly belong to this period, as do also Messrs. James and George Smillie, who have been equally happy in water and oil colors. The former is another of our

"SUNSET ON THE HUDSON."—[SANDFORD R. GIFFORD.]

many landscape-painters who began as engravers on steel. The later style of these talented brothers has been evidently modified with advantage by the influence of foreign technique, although they have studied wholly in this country; and they now display an attractive vigor and freshness in their landscape pieces, and a somewhat original choice of subjects.

The style of each of the artists we have mentioned can be distinguished at once. Individuality of expression is stamped upon the canvas of all; but among them there is no one more thoroughly original than Sanford R. Gifford, who, if he had lived in Persia or Peru two thousand years ago, might well have been an enthusiastic fire-worshipper, or daily welcomed the rising sun with reverent adoration. To him landscape-painting, whether of scenes in our own Far West, or on the legendary Hudson, or in the gorgeous East, has been alike the occasion for giving expression to his feeling for glowing atmospheric effects, for lyrics which on canvas reproduce the splendor of the sunset sky. But it would be a mistake to suppose that Mr. Gifford's poetic sense has been confined to the contemplation of serene and glowing atmospheres: he has also successfully rendered the lazy mist, the trailing vapor of morning enmeshed in dusky woodlands by the silent lake. His style combines to a remarkable degree deliberation and inspiration—a happy union of the analytical and emotional elements in art.

The objective school of American landscape-painting has found its culminating excellence, as it seems to us, in the art of Frederick E. Church. In his art-life the tendencies and aims of the chief national school we have produced during the last half century have been typically represented. In his works the technical weakness of this school is apparent, and, at the same time, its noble sympathy with nature, and its love for the grander aspects of the external world. It also represents the restless, unsatisfied genius of our people during this period, ever reaching out and beyond, and yearning, Venice-like, to draw to itself the spoils, the riches, the splendors, of the whole round globe. To our art the paintings of Mr. Church are what the geographic cantos of "Childe Harold" have been to the poesy of England, or the burning descriptions of St. Pierre and Chateaubriand to the literature of France. If such a topic is permissible in letters, may it not also be allowed sometimes in painting? Whether the one is as lofty as epic poetry, or the other as great as historical painting or subjective landscape, is a question which we do not need here to analyze. It is sufficient that each holds an important position; and to carry off the palm in either can only be the result of consummate genius. Yes! what "Childe Harold" did for the scenery of the Old World, the art of Church has done for that of the New. The vastness and the glory of this continent were yet unrevealed to us. With the enthusiasm of a Raleigh or a Balboa he has explored land and sea, combining the characteristics of the explorer and the artist. A pupil of Cole, he has carried to its full fruition the aspirations of his master, first gaining inspiration along the magical shores of the Hudson, and amidst the ideally beautiful ranges of the legendary Catskills. Our civilization needed exactly this form of art expression at this period, and the artist appeared who should teach the people to love beauty, and to find it among the regions which first rang with the axe of our pioneers.

But, although dealing not so much with nature, as such, as with some of her little known and more remarkable and startling effects, there is a very noteworthy absence of sensationalism or staginess in the paintings of Church; while, on the other hand, the somewhat too careful reproduction of details has not prevented them from possessing a grand massing of effect and a thrilling beauty and sublimity. "Cotopaxi," the "Heart of the Andes," or "Niagara," may transgress many rules laid down by the schools, but the magnificent ability with which they are represented dis-

A COMPOSITION.—[FREDERICK E. CHURCH.]

arms criticism. Church's first painting of Niagara occupies the culminating point in the objective art of this period of our history, executed by an artist who up to that time had never crossed the Atlantic, and whose merits and defects were entirely his own.

Mr. Church's "Niagara" is doubtless familiar to many through the fine chromo-lithographic copy made from it; but those who have not seen the original have only an incomplete idea of the grandeur of this great painting. It grows on acquaintance somewhat as does the cataract itself, until we seem to hear even the roar of the mighty waters that rushed over those tremendous cliffs ages before this continent was trodden by man, symbolizing the endless, remorseless, and irresistible sweep of time. The green flood pouring evermore into the appalling abyss veiled by mist wreathing up from the surging vortex below; the distant shore lined with foliage, touched by the burning tints of October; the rosy gray sky overarching the scene, and the ethereal bow uniting heaven and earth with its elusive band of colors—all are there, rendered with matchless art.

The subjects of Mr. Church's more recent works have been taken from the storied shores of the Mediterranean. We perceive in them no sign of failing power, but more breadth and less opulence of detail. The artist has treated the splendors of classic lands with the dignified reserve of matured strength and a higher sense of the ideal. The melancholy grandeur of the Parthenon in ruins has been painted with a stately reticence in consonance with the character of the subject; and the magnificent composition called the "Ægean" may well hold its own by the side of some of the superb Italian canvases of Turner.

A landscape-painter who chose a range of subjects similar to those of Church, and accompanied him in one of his South American trips, was Louis R. Mignot, of South Carolina, who died in London some eight years ago. He was inspired by a rapturous enthusiasm alike for the tender and the brilliant aspects of nature, and appears to us to have been one of the most remarkable artists of our country. He can be justly ranked with the pioneers who first awoke the attention of the nation to a consciousness of the beauty, glory, and inexhaustible variety of the scenery of this continent, which had fallen to them as a heritage such as no other people have yet acquired. Mignot was at once a fine colorist and one of the most skilled of our painters in the handling of materials; his was also a mind fired by a wide range of sympathies; and whether it was the superb splendor of the tropical scenery of the Rio Bamba, in South America, the sublime maddening rush of iris-circled water at Niagara, or the fairy-like grace, the exquisite and ethereal loveliness of new-fallen snow, he was equally happy in rendering the varied aspects of nature. It is greatly to be regretted that the most important works of this artist are owned in England, whither he resorted at the opening of the civil war. "Snow in Hyde Park," which he painted not long before his death, is one of the noblest productions of American landscape-painting.

"A WINTER SCENE."—[LOUIS R. MIGNOT.]

The American marine art of this period has been represented by a number of artists, although they have been by no means so numerous or capable as the maritime character of our people would have led us to expect. William Bradford, by origin a Quaker, has made to himself a name for his enterprise in going repeatedly to Labrador to study icebergs, and has executed some effective compositions, which have won him fame at home and abroad. Some of his coast scenes are also spirited, although open to the charge of technical errors. Charles Temple Dix, who unfortunately died young, painted some dashing, imaginative, and promising compositions; and Harry Brown, of Portland, has successfully rendered certain coast effects. But our ablest marine-painter of this period seems to have been James Hamilton, of Philadelphia, who was beyond question an artist of genius. His color was sometimes harsh and crude; but he handled pigments with mastery, and composed with the virile imagination of an improvisatore. Errors can doubtless be found in his ships, or the forms of his waves; but he was inspired by a genuine enthusiasm for the sea, and rendered the wildest and grandest effects of old ocean with breadth, massiveness, and power. We have had no marine-painter about whose works there is more of the raciness and flavor of blue water.

When we turn to the department of animal-painting, we discover what has been hitherto the weakest feature of American art, both in the number and quality of the artists who have pursued this branch of the profession. T. H. Hinckley at one time promised well in painting cattle and game, but his efforts rarely went beyond giving us Denner-like representations of stuffed foxes with glass eyes. The hairs were all there, the color was well enough, although perhaps a little foxy—if one may be permitted the term in this connection; but there was no life, no characterization, there. William Hayes showed decided ability in his representations of bisons and prairie-dogs and other dogs. Weak in color, he yet succeeded in giving spirit and character to the groups he painted, and holds among our animal-painters a position not dissimilar to that of Mount in *genre*.

Walter M. Brackett, who has been able rarely well to enjoy the triple

"SHIP OF 'THE ANCIENT MARINER.'"—[JAMES HAMILTON.]

pleasure of catching, painting, and eating the same fish on a summer's morning by the limpid brooks of New Hampshire, has justly won a reputation as an artistic Walton. If he would but paint his rocks and trees as cleverly as he renders the speckled monarch of the stream, his compositions would leave little to be desired. Henry C. Bispham has given us some spirited but sometimes badly drawn paintings of cattle and horses; and Colonel T. B. Thorpe, an amateur with artistic tastes, in such semi-humorous satires as "A Border Inquest," representing wolves sitting on the carcass of a buffalo, struck a vein peculiarly American in its humor, and carried to a high degree of excellence by William H. Beard, whose brother, James Beard, can also be justly ranked as an animal-painter of respectable attainments. Mr. Beard, although remarkably versatile, has made a specialty, if it may be so termed, of exposing the failings and foibles of our sinful humanity by the medium of animal *genre*. Monkeys, bears, goats, owls, and rabbits are in turn impressed into the benevolent service of taking us off, and repeating for us the old Spartan tale of the slave made drunk by his master as a warning to his son. Of the skill which Mr. Beard has exhibited in this novel line there can be no question. The "Dance of Silenus," the pertinacious, iterative, pragmatic ape called "The Bore," and "Bears on a Bender," are masterly bits of characterization. There is also a deal of comic satire in "The Bulls and Bears of Mammon's Fierce Zoology," which, with a multitude of struggling fighting figures, takes off the eccentricities of the Stock-exchange. Beard can justly be called the American Æsop. It is asserted by many that this is not art. The fact is that it is exceedingly difficult to draw the line, and to prescribe what subjects an artist shall choose. In art the result justifies the means. And this certainly seems as legitimate a subject for the brush of the artist as the graphic pictorial satires of Hogarth, or the mildly comical *genres* of Erskine Nicol.

In a previous chapter we alluded to some of the figure, historical, and *genre* painters of this period. William Mount was the precursor of a number of *genre* artists of more or less ability, among whom may be mentioned Thomas Hicks, a pupil of Couture, and one of the first of our painters who studied at Paris. In this admirable school Mr. Hicks became an excellent colorist, although of late his art has appeared to lose some of this quality. He has painted landscape and *genre*, meeting with respectable success in the latter, but portraiture has chiefly occupied his attention. His portrait of General Meade is a striking and satisfactory work. Then there was Richard Caton Woodville, who followed Whittredge to Düsseldorf, and promised much in *genre*. His paintings show very decided traces of German influence, but behind it all was a strong individuality that seemed destined to assert itself, and to place him among our foremost painters. But he died young, and (shall we not say?) happily for him, since little fame and less appreciation are destined to the artists who come ere the people are ripe for their art. George B. Flagg at one time promised well for our *genre* art, but his abilities were too precocious, and unfortunately the splendid opportunities he enjoyed as a pupil of All-

"WHOO!"—[WILLIAM H. BEARD.]

ston, and as a long resident in London, do not seem to have been sufficient to give growth or permanence to his talents.

About this time our frontier life was coming more prominently into view, and that picturesque border line between civilization and barbarism was becoming a subject for the pen of our leading writers. Irving, Cooper, and Kennedy, Street, Whittier, and Longfellow, were tuning the first efforts of their Muse to celebrate Indian life and border warfare in prose and verse, while the majestic measures of Bryant's "Prairies" seemed a prophetic prelude to the march of mankind toward the lands of the setting sun. "Evangeline," the most splendid result of our poetic literature, attracted not less for its magnificent generalizations of the scenery of the West than for the constancy of the heroine, and the artistic mind responded in turn to the unknown mystery and romance of that vast region, and gave us graphic pictures of the rude humanity which lent interest and sentiment to its unexplored solitudes. It is greatly to be regretted that the work of these pioneers in Western *genre* was not of more artistic value; from a historical point of view, too much importance cannot be attached to the enterprise and courage of men like Catlin, Deas, and Ranney, who, imbued with the spirit of adventure, identified themselves with Indian and border life, and rescued it from oblivion by their art enthusiasm, which, had it been guided by previous training, would have been of even greater value. As it is, they have with the pencil done a service for the subjects they portrayed similar to what Bret Harte has accomplished in giving immortality with the pen to the wild, picturesque, but evanescent mining scenes of the Pacific slope. In this connection the fact is worth recording that the important mutual life-insurance association called the Artists' Funding Society took its origin in a successful effort to contribute to the support of the family of Ranney after his death.

Our historical painters of this period rarely created any works deserving of note or remembrance. Here and there a painting like that of Huntington's "Republican Court" was produced, which is a graceful and elegant composition, and one of the best of the kind in American art. Peter F. Rothermel, the able portrait-painter of Philadelphia, also composed a number of historical works, of which the last is probably of most value. His "Battle of Gettysburg" is a bold and not ineffective representation of one of the critical moments in the world's history, although open in parts to severe criticism. J. G. Chapman, well known at one time as a skilful wood-engraver and *genre* painter, also aspired to the difficult field of historical painting; but it is to an artist of German extraction, Emmanuel Leutze, that we owe our best historical art previous to 1860, excepting perhaps some of the compositions of Copley and West and two or three of the battle-pieces of Trumbull. Although born abroad, Leutze may be justly claimed as an American painter, for he was taken to Philadelphia in childhood, and remained in this country until thoroughly imbued with a patriotic love for the land and its history and the spirit of its institutions; and although he subsequently passed a number of years at Dusseldorf, whither he went at twenty-seven, the last ten years of his life were here; here he died, and the subjects of his art were almost entirely inspired by American scenes, and have become incorporated with the growth of our civilization.

Leutze was a man who was cast in a large mould, capable of a grand enthusiasm, and aspiring to grasp soaring ideals. Although his art was often at fault, it makes us feel, notwithstanding, that in contemplating his works we are in the presence of a colossal mind which, under healthier influences, would have better achieved what he aspired to win. He drew

"LAFAYETTE IN PRISON."—[E. LEUTZE.]

from wells of seemingly inexhaustible inspiration. He was Byronic in the impetus of his genius, the rugged incompleteness of his style, the magnificent fervor and rush of his fancy, the epic grandeur and energy, dash and daring, of his creations. It is easy to say that he was steeped in German conventionalism, that he pictured the impossible, that he was sometimes harsh in his color and technique; and so he was at times, but, with it all, he left the impression of vast intellectual resources.

We would not be understood as saying that all the works of Leutze are worthy of unqualified acceptance; we refer rather to their general character. His art was very prolific, and as a pupil of Lessing and Schadow it bore the unmistakable stamp of Düsseldorf. Much of his work, partaking also of the grandiose style of Kaulbach, was of a semi-decorative character, like the "Landing of the Norsemen," which represents two fresh, sturdy Scandinavian rovers stepping out of an impossible ship, bearing aloft a noble princess, and in the very act of landing snatching the grapes "hanging wanton to be plucked." Spirited as it is, the manifest absurdity of the composition as a representation of reality yet requires us to accept it as decorative in design. "Godiva" is a somewhat coarse but characteristic work of Leutze, and the "Iconoclast" one of his most interesting and artistic works. In America, Leutze will be remembered longest by his large and magnificent painting of "Washington at Princeton," his "Emigration to the West" (a decorative composition in one of the panels of the stairway of the Capitol at Washington), and his "Washington Crossing the Delaware." The latter was executed at Düsseldorf, and the ice was painted from an unusual mass of shattered ice floating down the Rhine on the breaking up of the winter. It is another illustration of the apparent caprice with which man is treated by destiny, that scarcely had Leutze closed his eyes in his last sleep, at the early age of fifty-one, when a letter arrived from Germany bringing official tidings that he had just been elected to succeed Lessing as president of the Düsseldorf Academy of Art.

While we find in Leutze the qualities we have described, it cannot be said that he sought out any new methods of expression, or that he undertook to suggest the deeper and more subtle traits of human nature; he was content to work after the manner of the school in which he studied. It is to another painter (already referred to), of great intellectual resource and a thoroughly American discontent with the actual, that we turn for aspirations after a higher form of art. William Page, a native of Albany, who studied law, and for a time also theology, at Andover Seminary, was from the first biassed in favor of art. His mind presents a combination of the speculative and the practical, and it is the union of these antithetical qualities which has alternately aided or hindered the success of Page's efforts and experiments. He is deliberate rather than inspirational, guided by an exquisite feeling for color and an admirable sense of form, but too often unduly controlled by the logical and analytical faculty. Had his fancy only been more childlike, and been left more to the guidance of

its own natural and correct instincts. Mr. Page's works would have oftener moved us by their beauty rather than by the dexterity of the technique. Still, it is by the aid of a few such questioning minds that art makes its advances, and interprets the secrets of nature. As a portrait painter, Page has placed himself among the first artists of the age. We see in his portraits a dignity and repose, a grasp of character, and a harmonious richness of color that are wonderfully impressive. In attempting to represent the beauty of the feminine figure Mr. Page has been influenced by great

"THE REFUGE."—[ELIHU VEDDER.]

delicacy and refinement of motive, although in the celebrated painting of "Venus Rising from the Sea," he gave cause for much discussion as to the merits of his theories.

When Page was in his prime, our literature had already become distinguished by several writers of thoroughly original and mystically creative imagination, native to the soil, and drawing sustenance from native inspiration: they were Charles Brockden Brown, Judd, Hawthorne, and Poe. In point of originality in conceiving of scenes powerfully weird and imaginative, these writers have had no superiors in this century. With a style essentially individual, they analyzed the workings of the human heart, and dealt with the great problems of destiny. Their genius was cosmopolitan, and for all ages. Our pictorial art, in a less degree, began soon after to be prompted by a similar tendency.

Most prominent among these artists whose faltering efforts have most distinctly articulated the language and aspirations of the soul are Elihu Vedder and John Lafarge. It cannot be said that either of these artists has yet accomplished with complete success the end he has sought; but their efforts have been in the right direction, and as such are highly interesting, hopeful, and suggestive.

Mr. Vedder's early *genre* and landscape compositions are full of subtle attempts at psychology in color. Outward nature with him is but a means for more effectively conveying the impressions of humanity; and his faces are full of vague, mystic, far-off searching after the infinite, and the why and the wherefore of this existence below. Since Mr. Vedder took up his residence permanently in Italy, he has improved in technique, and there is less dryness in his method of using color, as witnessed by his remarkable painting called a "Venetian Dancing Girl, or 'La Regina;'" but he has not in recent years produced anything so marvellously imaginative as his "Lair of the Sea-Serpent," or so grand and desolate as his "Death of Abel." The man who painted the "Lost Mind," the "Death of Abel," and the "Lair of the Sea-Serpent," did not need to borrow from the ancients—at least so far as regards forms of expression. The vast, solemn, appalling solitude of the primeval world, the terrific sublimity of its first tragedy, are rendered in Mr. Vedder's painting with the sombre grandeur of Dante; while as a work of imaginative art, the steel-colored monster reposing his gigantic folds on the dry grass of a desolate shore by the endless seas, is a composition of wonderful simplicity and mysterious power, a creation of pure genius.

Mr. Lafarge is by nature a colorist; to color, the emotional element of art, his sensitive nature vibrates as to well-attuned harmonies of music. For form he has less feeling; his drawing is often very defective, and the lines are hesitating, uncertain, and feeble. But we have had no artist since Stuart who has shown such a natural sympathy for the shades and modulations of chromatic effects. But, while his drawing is open to criticism, this artist is inspired by the general meaning of form, and has sometimes produced some very weird and startling compositions entirely in

CARTOON SKETCH: CHRIST AND NICODEMUS.—[JOHN LAFARGE.]

black and white, or camaieu. But whether it be form or color, the various elements of art are regarded by Lafarge not so much for what they are as for what they suggest; he is less concerned with the external than with the hidden meaning it has for the soul. It is because of his subtle way of regarding the beauty of this world that he has given us such thoughtful landscapes as "Paradise at Newport," and such exquisitely painted flowers, rendered with a tender harmony of color that thrills us like a lyric of

Keats or of Tennyson. It is this serious, reflective turn which has given a religious hue to his art, and has enabled him to succeed so well in the most ambitious attempt at decorative-painting yet undertaken in this country—the frescoes of Trinity Church, in Boston: in which, it should be added, he was ably assisted by Mr. Lathrop. In these compositions we see the results of a highly ideal and reverent nature, nourished by the most abundant art opportunities the age could afford. It is not difficult to find in them points fairly open to attack; but the promise they show is so hopeful a sign in our art, the success actually achieved in them in a direction quite new in this country is so marked, that we prefer to leave to others any unfavorable criticism they may suggest.

IV.

AMERICAN PAINTERS.

1828-1878.

THE discovery of the gold mines of California was a signal for enterprise, daring, and achievement, not only to our commerce and the thrift of our shifting millions of uneasy settlers, but also to the literature and landscape-art of the United States. "To the kingdom of the west wind" hied artist and author alike; and the epic of the settlement of California, of the scaling of the Rocky Mountains, of the glory of the Columbia River, and the stupendous horrors of the Yellowstone was pictured on the canvas of the artist. Taylor and Scott conquered the Pacific slope; Fremont pointed out the pathway over the swelling ranges of the Sierras; and our painters revealed to us the matchless splendor of a scenery which shall arouse increasing astonishment and reverential awe and rapture in the hearts of generations yet to be. In the gratitude we owe to these landscape-painters who dared, discovered, and delineated for us the scenery of which we were hitherto the ignorant possessors, criticism is almost left in abeyance, for the service done the people has been a double one—in leading them to the observation of paintings, and informing them of the attractions of a little known possession. If the art of these paintings of our Western scenery had been in all respects equal to the subject, the country would have been rich indeed. Among the artist explorers to whom we are most indebted, Messrs. Bierstadt, Hill, and Moran are the most famous. The former, by his great composition entitled the "Rocky Mountains," threw the people into an ecstasy of delight, which at this time it is difficult to understand, and bounded at one step to celebrity.

Albert Bierstadt is a native of Düsseldorf, but came to this country in infancy. Subsequently he studied at Düsseldorf and Rome. On returning to America, he accompanied the exploring expedition of General Lander that went over the plains in 1858. Fitz Hugh Ludlow, the well-known *littérateur*, was associated with him in a subsequent trip, and several graphic articles in which he afterward described the journey undoubtedly helped to bring Mr. Bierstadt into notice.

The "Rocky Mountains" is not the representation of an actual scene, but a typical composition, and, thus regarded, is an interesting work, although it seems to us somewhat too theatrical, and scarcely true in some of the details. Local truth is desirable in topographical art, although of quite secondary importance in compositions of a more ideal character. Since then this artist has executed a number of similarly ambitious paintings of our Western scenery, including a colossal painting of the gorge of the Yosemite Valley. All of them are characterized by boldness of treatment, but sometimes they are crude in color and out of tone. Of these we prefer, as least sensational and most artistically correct, the painting of a storm on Mount Rosalie. Bierstadt's smaller California scenes are generally more valuable than his large ones for artistic quality: one of the best compositions we have seen from his easel is a war sketch representing Federal sharp-shooters on the crest of a hill behind some trees. This is an excellent piece of work, fresh, original, and quite free from the Düsseldorf taint; and confirms us in the opinion that Mr. Bierstadt is naturally an artist of great ability and large resources, and might easily have maintained a reputation as such if he had not grafted on the sensationalism of Düsseldorf a greater ambition for notoriety and money than for success in pure art.

Some of the qualities we have learned to look for in vain in the canvases of Bierstadt we find emphasized in the paintings of Thomas Hill, who succeeded him as court painter to the monarch of the Rocky Mountains. Hill began life as a coach-painter at Taunton, Massachusetts. After deciding on a professional art career, he visited Europe, and benefited by observation in foreign studios, especially of France, although his style is essentially his own. His method of using pigments is sometimes open to the accusation of hardness; there is too often a lack of juiciness— a dryness that seems to remind us of paint rather than atmosphere, which may be owing to the fact, as I have been informed, that he uses little or no oil in going over a painting the second time. But Mr. Hill is a good colorist, bold and massive in his effects, and a very careful, conscientious student of nature. He has been happy in the rendering of wood interiors,

"VIEW ON THE KERN RIVER."—[A. BIERSTADT.]

as, for example, bits from the Forest of Fontainebleau. One of his most remarkable New England landscapes represents the avalanche in the Notch of the White Mountains, which was attended with such disastrous results to the dwellers in the valley. But Mr. Hill will be identified in future with California, where he has become a resident, and has devoted his energies to painting some of the magnificent scenery of that marvellous region, where the roar of the whirlwind and the roll of the thunder reverberate like the tread of the countless millions who evermore march to the westward. As he sat on the edge of the precipice, the forerunner of coming ages, and painted the sublime, solitary depths of the Yosemite, did the artist realize that with every stroke of the brush he was aiding the advance guard of civilization, and driving away the desolation which gave additional grandeur to one of the most extraordinary spots on the planet? In his great painting of the Yosemite he seems to have been inspired by a reverential spirit; he has taken no liberties with his subject, but has endeavored with admirable art to convey a correct impression of the scene; and the work may be justly ranked with the best examples of the American school of landscape-painting.

The first fever of the California rush had subsided when the uneasy explorer again stirred the enthusiasm of adventurous artists by thrilling descriptions of the Yellowstone River, its Tartarean gorges, and the lurid splendor of its sulphurous cliffs and steaming geysers. Once more the landscape artist of the country was moved to go forth and make known

"THE YOSEMITE."—[THOMAS HILL.]

to us those unrevealed wonders; and Thomas Moran, "taking his life in his hands," in the language of religious cant, aspired to capture the bouquet, the first bloom, from this newly-opened draught of inspiration.

"THE BATHERS."—[THOMAS MORAN.]

We all know the result. Who has not seen his splendid painting of the "Gorge of the Yellowstone," now in the Capitol at Washington? Granting the fitness of the subject for art, it can be frankly conceded that this is one of the best paintings of the sort yet produced. The vivid local colors of the rocks, which there is no reason to doubt have been faithfully rendered—for Mr. Moran is a careful and indefatigable student of certain phases of nature—appear, however, to give such works a sensational effect.

This seems to us to be the most valuable of the numerous paintings of Western subjects produced by this artist. It would be a mistake, however, to judge him wholly by the more ambitious compositions suggested by tropical or Western scenery. Some of his ideal paintings are very clever, and show us an ardent student of nature, and a mind inspired by a fervid imagination. But while conceding thus much to the talents of this artist—who belongs to an artistic family, two of his brothers being also well-known painters, one in marine, the other in cattle painting—we cannot accord him great original powers. He has studied the technique of his calling most carefully, and has bestowed great attention to the methods of several celebrated artists; but we are too often conscious, in looking at his works, that his style has leaned upon that of certain favorite painters. There is great cleverness, but little genius, apparent in the landscapes of Mr. Moran, for the imitative faculty has been too much for him.

Contemporary with our school of grand nature, if we may so call it, and represented by artists native in thought and education, we find evidences of another beginning to assert itself, of altogether a different character. The former deals wholly with externals, and the subject is the first end sought; it concerns itself altogether with objects, and not with any ulterior thoughts which they may suggest to the sensitive imagination. The latter, on the other hand, searches out the mystery in nature, and analyzes its human aspects. It is the vague suggestions seen in hills and skies, in sere woods and lonely waters, and moorlands fading away into eternity—it is their symbolism and sympathy with the soul that an artist like Mr. Jervis M'Entee seeks to represent on canvas. This is, in a word, the subjective art to which we have already alluded. To him the voice of nature is an elegy; the fall of the leaves in October suggests the passing away of men to the grave in a countless and endless procession; and whenever he introduces the agency of man into his pictures, it is as if he were fighting with an unseen and remorseless destiny. Exquisitely poetic and beautiful are the autumnal scenes of this artist, the reaches of russet woodlands, the expanses of skurrying clouds, gray, melancholy, wild. His art sings in a low minor key that finds response in the heart of multitudes who have suffered, to whom the world has been a battle-field, where the

LANDSCAPE.—[JERVIS M'ENTEE.]

losses have outweighed the gains, and have left them gazing into the mysterious future like one who at midnight stands on the brink of a tremendous abyss into which he must be hurled, but knows not what are the shuddering possibilities that await the inevitable plunge.

A young artist of Boston died in Syria, four years ago, at the early age of twenty-five, before he had acquired more than local repute, who gave promise of standing among the foremost of American landscape-painters. I refer to A. P. Close. Certainly no artist we have produced has evinced more abundant signs of genius at so early an age. Nor was he wholly a landscape-painter; the figure was also one aim of his art, and it was in the combination of the two that he excelled. He also had an eye for color that has not been too common in our art; and, wholly untaught, expressed his moods and fancies with a force that, even in its immaturity, suggested the master. But the one point in which he surpassed most of our artists up to this time was in the singular and inexhaustible activity of the imaginative faculty. It is strange that one so young should have so early manifested in his art a serious, almost morbid, view of life. It may have been because he found himself, before the age of twenty, forced to provide for a fatherless family, and to devote the greater part of his energies to what was to him the uncongenial work of drawing on wood.

Less subjective and morbid, but moved by a similar feeling for the suggestions of nature, A. H. Wyant displays a sympathy with scenery and a masterful skill in reaching subtle effects which place him among the first landscape-painters of the age. In the suggestive rendering of space and color, of the manifold phases of a bit of waste land, or mountain glen, or sedgy brook-side, simple enough at first sight, but full of an infinitude of unobtrusive beauty, he works with the magic of a high-priest of nature; his style is broad in effect, without being slovenly and careless, and gives a multitude of details while really dealing chiefly with

"COUNTY KERRY."—[A. H. WYANT.]

one central and prevailing idea. Mr. Wyant's work occasionally shows traces of foreign influences; but he is an artist of too much original power to be under any necessity to stunt himself by the imitation of the style of any other artist, however great.

Homer Martin is another painter who views nature for the sentiment it suggests, while he is impressed chiefly by color and light; for form he seems to have less feeling. But he is a lyrist with the brush, and his sympathy with certain aspects of nature is akin to idolatry. With a few intense and telling strokes, he brings before us the splendors of sunset or the quietude of twilight, the gray vapors of morning creeping over dank woodlands or the sublime pathos of lonely sands, haunted by wild fowl and beaten by the hollow seas. But we have no painter whose art is so unequal: in all his works there is absolute freedom, freshness, and originality; his scheme of color is altogether his own, full of luminousness and purity; but he is weak in technique, and thus he alternately startles us by the brilliance, beauty, and suggestiveness of one painting, and the palpable failure to reach the desired end in another. However, this very irregularity in achievement shows that he is subject to inspirations, and thus partakes of the character of genius, which, if it were of a higher order, would be more often successful in its attempts.

In the works of these painters we see abundant reason to believe in the permanent vitality of American landscape art, and evidence that it is not inclined to run in a conventional groove. Just so long as the artists who represent it continue to assert their individuality with such nerve and keen perception of the essential truths of nature, art is in a healthy and progressive condition. If further evidence of this were needed, we might cite the landscapes of J. Appleton Brown, who, after a rather discouraging servitude to Corôt, is at last beginning to show us the reserve power of which he is capable when he is more concerned with nature than with imitating the style and thoughts of another. Ernest Longfellow, a son of the poet, is another exemplar of the sturdy and healthful personality which everywhere crops out in our landscape art. While it cannot be said that his paintings suggest greatness, they breathe a true spirit, and possess a purity of color that is very attractive.

D. W. C. Boutelle, long resident at Bethlehem, Pennsylvania, and rarely exhibiting in public in late years, is well known by such works as "The Trout Brook Shower" and engravings of other paintings by him, as an artist of originality and force, who seems to combine in his style some of the best traits of the American School of landscape-painting.

E. M. Bannister, of Providence, is also a man of genius. In the matter of drawing he is weak; but, although he has never been abroad, we

"THE ADIRONDACKS."—[HOMER MARTIN.]

recognize in his treatment of masses, and the brilliance of his method of managing light and color, the progressive transition through which our landscape art is passing, even when it does not pay allegiance to foreign influences.

Our marine art of the last fifteen years has shown that the illimitable aspects of the sea are also receiving increased attention, and are calling

A LANDSCAPE.—[J. W. CASILEAR.]

forth some of the best art talent of the country. It may be partly due to the advent of M. F. H. De Haas, who came here from Holland already an accomplished artist, who had done so well in his native land as to be appointed court painter to the queen. An artist of brilliant parts, although sometimes inclined to sensationalism, he has undoubtedly created some splendid compositions; and his influence must have been of decided importance during this period. While he has been working in New York, two marine painters of Boston have also executed some striking and beautiful works. I refer to John E. C. Petersen and William E. Norton. The former died young, in 1876. He was by birth a Dane, and in personal appearance a viking: tall, handsome, tawny-haired, with a clear, sharp blue eye, and a bearing that reminded one of an admiral on the quarter-deck of his frigate swooping down with flying sheets across the enemy's bow and pouring in a raking fire. Those who have seen him will never forget the grand figure of Petersen, the very impersonation of a son of the sea. When he first began to paint in Boston his pictures were weak in color and rude in drawing. But he improved with marvellous rapidity, and at the time of his death had few peers in marine art. Every inch a sailor, to him a ship was no clumsy mass laid awkwardly on the top of the water, as too many painters represent it, but a thing of life, with an individuality of its own, graceful as a queen, and riding the waves like a swan. "Making Sail after a Storm," representing a clipper ship shaking out her top-sails in the gray gloom that succeeds a storm, and rising massively but easily against the sky on the crest of the weltering seas, is a very strong picture. So also is his "After the Collision," and "A Ship Running before a Squall." When shall we see his like again?

Mr. Norton began life as a house-painter, and is related to a family of ship-builders. He has himself made several voyages before the mast, and is therefore well equipped, so far as observation goes. He has painted many works, sometimes with more rapidity than comports with artistic success; and his style is occasionally hard, mannered, and mechanical. But he is an enthusiast for his art, and sometimes a happy inspiration enables him to turn off a painting that entitles him to a high rank among the marine painters of the age. He has been most happy in quiet effects and fog scenes, and a composition called the "Fog-Horn," representing two men in a dory blowing a horn to warn away a steamer that is stealthily approaching them out of the fog, is a very interesting work. "Crossing the Grand Banks" is the title of another painting by this artist, in which the luminous haze of a midday fog and a large ship threading her way through a fleet of fishing-schooners, are rendered with a truth of color and majesty of form that give this work an important position in contemporary American art.

Inferior to these artists as a draughtsman or in knowledge of ships,

Arthur Quartley has, however, won a rapid and deserved reputation for coast scenes and effects of shimmering light on still water. Prettiness rather than beauty is sometimes too evident in his work; but he composes with decided originality, showing a real passion for the effects after

"SHIP ASHORE."—[M. F. H. DE HAAS.]

which he strives, and his skies are often very strong. A "Storm off the Isles of Shoals" is one of his most important compositions. Mr. Lansil, of Boston, seems to be practically ignorant of the first principles of drawing and perspective, but he has shown a feeling for color and light, and we have at present few artists who equal him in painting still harbor scenes, marbled with reflections wavering on a glassy surface. Among our more clever coast painters we cannot omit the mention of A. T. Bricher, who renders certain familiar scenes of the Atlantic shore with much realistic force, but little feeling for the ideal. J. C. Nicoll seems to show more promise in this direction. The color and technique of his pictures are very clever and interesting, and well illustrate the sea as it looks to a landsman from *terra firma*. Both of these artists have painted extensively in *aquarelle*, in which medium they have achieved some important results; which may justly be added regarding the marine paintings of F. A. Silva. As a water-colorist Mr. Nicoll is not excelled by any of our artists now concerned with coast scenes; and some of his landscapes in *aquarelle* sometimes rival his marines. What we observe in most of our marine-painters, however, is weakness in the matter of original composition. One would think that no object in nature would stimulate the imagination and expand the mind more than the sea. But it does not seem to have that effect in our marine art as yet, excepting here and there a solitary instance.

No fact better attests the active and prosperous character of American art than the rapid success which the culture of water-colors has achieved among us. In 1865 a collection of English water-color paintings was brought to this country, and exhibited in New York. It attracted much attention; and although a few artists, like Messrs. Parsons and Falconer, had already used this medium here, generally as amateurs, this seems to have been the first occasion that stimulated our artists to follow the art of water-color painting seriously. A society, headed by such men as Messrs. Samuel Colman, G. Burling, well known notwithstanding his early

"A FOGGY MORNING."—[W. E. NORTON.]

death, as a painter of game birds, J. M. Falconer, and R. Swain Gifford, was formed within a year; Mr. Colman was the first president, and the first annual exhibition was held in the halls of the Academy of Design in 1867. Twelve exhibitions have now been held, and Messrs. James

Smillie and T. W. Wood have in turn succeeded Mr. Colman in the presidency. A numerous school of artists has sprung up, finding expression wholly in water-colors, like Miss Susan Hale or Henry Farrar, the able landscape-painter; while many of our leading artists in landscape and *genre* have learned in this short period to work with equal success in *aquarelle* and oil. The later exhibitions have been characterized by an individuality and strength that compare most favorably with the exhibitions of the older societies of London.

Another interesting feature of the last part of the period under consideration is the increasing attention bestowed on the drawing of the figure. The number of *genre* artists has notably increased; and the quality of their work has, on the whole, been on a higher plane. The war gave an impetus to this department, with its many sad or comic situations, and the increasing immigration of the peasantry of Europe, and the growing variety of our national types and street scenes, have all contributed to attract and stimulate the artistic eye and fancy. To mention all the artists among us who have, especially of late, achieved more or less success in this line, would be to enumerate a long catalogue, and we must content ourselves with the brief mention of a few who seem, perhaps, to be the most noteworthy, and, at the same time, indigenous in their style.

J. B. Irving, who has but recently passed away, executed some very clever cabinet compositions, delicately drawn and painted, somewhat in the modern French style, generally interiors, with figures in old-time costume. A very favorable specimen of his work is represented in a painting entitled "The End of the Game." B. F. Mayer, of Annapolis, has also devoted himself to a similar class of subjects successfully. He is, however, very versatile, and gives us at will a gentleman in Louis Quatorze costume, elaborately painted, or a bluff tar on the forecastle on the lookout, or aloft tarring down the rigging, or a religious ceremonial in the wigwams of the North-west. Marcus Waterman, of Providence, has displayed much dash in *genre* combined with landscape, and is fresh and vigorous in style; while such a carefully executed work as his "Gulliver at Lilliput" is highly creditable to our art. J. W. Champney studied abroad under Frère, and also at Antwerp, and is one of the most broad-minded of our younger artists; indeed, it is refreshing to meet an artist so unbiassed by prejudice. His foreign studies have in no wise narrowed his intellectual sympathies. His small *genre* compositions, especially of child life, often together with landscape, have been carefully finished—latterly with an especial regard to the values. Professor John F. Weir, who comes of an artistic family, and is Superintendent of the Academy of Art at New

A MARINE.—[ARTHUR QUARTLEY.]

Haven, has shown capacity and nerve in his well-known painting called "Forging the Shaft," forcibly representing one of the most striking incidents in a foundry; and A. W. Willard, of Cincinnati, has struck out in a similar vein. Energy of action, and an effort after effect verging on exaggeration and caricature, are the characteristics of the style with which he has attempted such novel compositions as "Yankee Doodle" and "Jim Bludsoe." They suggest in color the literature of Artemus Ward and Walt Whitman. At the same time, we recognize in such thorough individuality a very promising attempt to assert the possibilities of certain phases of our national *genre*. These traits have been treated with less daring but with more artistic success by two of our best-known *genre* painters—T. W. Wood and J. G. Brown. Mr. Wood, who is president of the Water-color Society, and employs both oil and water colors, spent several of the first years of his career at the South, and discovered of what importance our colored citizens might prove in our art—their squalor, picturesqueness, broad and kindly humor, and the pathos which has invested their fate with unusual interest. This artist's first successful venture in *genre* was with a painting of a quaint old negro at Baltimore; and since then he has given us many characteristic compositions suggested by the lot of the slave, although he has not confined himself to this subject, but has also picked up excellent subjects among the newsboys in our streets, and amidst the homespun scenes of rural life. Mr. Wood's style is notable for *chiar-oscuro*, and his drawing is generally careful, correct, and forcible, and his compositions harmonious.

Mr. Brown has also found that success and fame in *genre* can be obtained without going abroad to seek for subjects. To him the *gamins* of our cities are as artistically attractive as those of Paris, and a girl wandering by our sea-shore as winsome as if on the beach at Nice or Scheveningen, and an old fisherman at Grand Menan as pictorial as if he were under the cliffs at Etretât. Fault is sometimes found with the fact that the street lads painted by Mr. Brown have always washed their faces before posing, which is according to the commands of St. Paul, but not of art canons, if we accept Mr. Ruskin's dictum regarding the artistic value of dirt. Bating this apparently trifling difficulty, however, it must be admitted that he often offers us a very characteristic and successful bit of *genre*. Gilbert Gaul and J. Burns, pupils of Mr. Brown, merit a word of praise in this connection, for giving us reason to hope in time for some satisfactory work from their easels.

Child life finds a warm friend and delineator in S. J. Guy, who has made many friends by the kindly way in which he has treated the simple pathos and humor of childhood. He is an admirable draughtsman, and finishes his work with great nicety—sometimes to a degree that seems to rob the picture of some of its freshness and piquancy; but it cannot be denied that Mr. Guy has often struck a chord in the popular heart, not merely by his choice of subjects, but by legitimately earned success in his art as well. Scenes of domestic life have also been treated sometimes very interestingly by Messrs. B. F. Reinhart, Ehninger, Blauvelt, Satterlee, Howland, Wilmarth, and Virgil Williams. Oliver J. Lay, although a slow, careful artist, has executed some thoughtful and refined in-door scenes, taken from domestic life, which show a thorough appreciation of the fact that art, for itself alone, is the only aim the true artist should pursue. E. L. Henry surprises one by the elaboration of his work, and is open to the charge of crudeness in color and hardness in outline; but occasionally he gives us a well-balanced composition, like the beach scene, with horses and a carry-all in the foreground, entitled "Waiting for the Bathers."

"ARGUING THE QUESTION."—[T. W. WOOD.]

But it is in the works of Messrs. Eastman Johnson and Winslow Homer that we find the most successful rendering of American *genre* of the present day as distinguished from that which bears unmistakable evidence of foreign inspiration. Mr. Johnson, as a student at Düsseldorf and other art centres of Europe, might be expected to show the fact in his art; but, instead of doing so, we have no painter who has a more individual style. There is uncertainty in his drawing sometimes, but his color and composition are generally excellent, and the choice of subjects are at the same time popular and artistic. We have had no painter since Mount who has done more to elevate the character of *genre* art in the community. Successful in portraiture and ideal heads, Mr. Johnson has achieved his best efforts in the homely scenes of rustic negro life, or from a thorough sympathy with the simplicity and beauty of childhood. None who have seen his painting called the "Old Stage-Coach," representing a rollicking group of boys and girls playing on the rusty wreck of an abandoned mail-carriage, can ever doubt again the possibilities of *genre* art in this country, although some of his simpler compositions are more to our liking. There is, however, nothing startling or especially novel in the style of Mr. Johnson. It is quiet and unsensational.

It is to the eccentric and altogether original compositions of Winslow Homer that we turn for a more decided expression of the growing weariness of our people with the conventional, and a vague yearning after an original form of art speech. The freshness, the crudity, and the solid worth of American civilization are well typified in the thoroughly native art of Mr. Homer. No artist has shown more versatility and inventiveness in choice of subject, and greater impatience with accepted methods. Impatience, irritability, is written upon all his works — he is evidently striving after the unknown. But the key-note of his art seems to be a realistic endeavor to place man and nature, landscape and *genre*, in harmonious juxtaposition; never one alone, but both aiding each other, they are ever the themes of his brush. His figures are often stiff or posed in awkward attitudes, and yet they always arrest the attention, for they are inspired by an active, restless brain, that is undoubtedly moved by the impulse of genius. It is the values, or true relations of objects as they actually appear in nature, that this artist also seeks to render; while in his reach after striking subjects or compositions he not rarely borders on the sensational. But in some of his masterly water-color sketches, which are almost impressionist in treatment, or such more finished works as "The Cotton Pickers," a scene from Southern plantation life, Mr. Homer asserts his right to be considered the founder of a new school of *genre* painting. The repose which is lacking in his style at present may come to him later, or be grafted upon it by those who come after him.

George Fuller, of Boston, is another artist in whose works we see an additional proof of the growing importance attached to the painting of the figure in our art. His paintings indicate the presence among us of a vigorous, original personality, that is, of a genius striving for utterance. They are incomplete, rarely altogether satisfactory; but we feel, in the presence of such a subtle, suggestive, mysterious composition as the "Rommany Girl," vaguely thrilling us with the deep meaning of her weirdly glancing eyes, and weaving a mystic spell over our fancy, that a mind akin to that of Hawthorne is here striving for utterance, and unconsciously infusing new vitality into our *genre* art.

As an influence in the same direction, the compositions of William Magrath command sincere attention. It is not so many years ago since he was painting signs in New York, and now we see him one of the strongest artists in *genre* on this side of the Atlantic. Mr. Magrath generally paints single figures, associated with rural life—a milkmaid, or a farmer. Naturally there is inequality in the results achieved, and sometimes manifest weakness. But we note a constant progress in the quality of his art, and an evidence of imagination which has been unfortunately too rare in American *genre* since the days of William Mount. By this we mean the

"THE ROSE."—[D. F. MAYER.]

identification of the artist with his subject, which renders it dramatic, and inspires it with that touch of nature that makes the whole world kin. In this respect he occasionally suggests the inimitable humanity which is the crowning excellence of the paintings of Jean François Millet.

It is with additional pleasure that we note the works of some of our more recent native *genre* artists, because we see indicated in them a growing perception of the fact that abundant subjects may be found at our own doors to occupy the pencil of the ablest minds. It is not uncommon to hear young artists who have studied in the ateliers of Paris and Munich, and who have returned here to work, complaining that they find no sources of inspiration here, no subjects to paint at home. This dearth of subjects certainly would be a very grave obstacle to the ultimate development of a great American school of art, if it actually existed. But on examining the question, it seems to us that the difficulty lies not in the lack of subjects, but in the way the artist has learned to look at things, and the range of sympathies to which he has become accustomed by his foreign experiences.

The artist who is the man of his time and his country never yet lacked material for inspiration in the every-day life and every-day objects around him. Goethe has said that the truest poetry is that woven out of the suggestions gained from simple things. There has never yet been such a state of society or such an order of scenery that the artist who was in sympathy with it could not find some poetry, some color, some form or light or shade in it that would stir the finer elements of his genius, stimulate his fancy, and arouse his inventive powers. Some quality of beauty is there, concealed like the water in the rock; the magician comes whose rod can evoke the imprisoned element, and others then see what he had first seen.

As we stroll, for example, through the streets and squares of New York's metropolis, by its teeming wharves, and among its dilapidated avenues of trade, we are astounded to think that any one could ever look on this seething mass of humanity, these various types of man, and the various structures he has erected here, and find in them no inspiration for his brush or his pen. What if there are no feluccas or painted sails in our harbor; one has but to cross the river on the ferry-boat at sunrise or sunset to see wonderful picturesqueness and beauty in our sloops and schooners, our shipping thronging the piers, all smitten by the glory of the rosy light, or over-canopied by scowling gray masses of storm-driven scud.

Or if one saunters up our streets and gazes on the long vista of Broadway toward nightfall, as the lazy mist gradually broods over the roofs and delicately tones and softens the receding rows of buildings, he shall see effects almost as entrancing and poetic as those which charm the enthusiast who beholds the sun, a crimson disk, couching in a gray bank of smoke at the end of the boulevards of Paris, on an evening in October.

Is there nothing picturesque and artistic in the Italian fruit venders at the street corners, especially when after dark they light their smoking torches, that waver with ruddy glow over brilliant masses of oranges and apples?

There is yet another scene which we often encounter, especially early in the morning, at a time when perhaps most artists are yet wrapped in dreams. We refer to the groups of horses led through the streets to the horse-market. Untrimmed, unshorn, massively built, and marching in files

"DRESS PARADE."—[J. G. BROWN.]

by fours and fives with clanging tread, sometimes thirty or forty together, they present a stirring and powerful effect, which would thrill a Bonheur or a Schreyer. Why have none of our artists attempted to paint them? Have we none with the knowledge or the power to render the subject with the vigor it demands?

No, we lack not subjects for those who know how to see them; while nothing is more certain than the truth that a national art can only be founded and sustained by those who are wholly in sympathy with the influences of the land whose art they are aiding to establish. Those who are familiar with American art will easily recall a number of our artists,

"A BED-TIME STORY."—[S. J. GUY.]

THE MOTHER.—[EASTMAN JOHNSON.]

educated both at home and abroad, who have no difficulty in finding material around home, and at the same time take the lead among us in point of artistic strength.

While indicating, however, some of the many subjects which address one at every turn in our land, and render it unnecessary for artists to go abroad for a supply of fuel for their fancy, we would not, on the other hand, imply that an artist should, in order to be an exponent or leader of a native art, be confined exclusively to one class of subjects. Although it is one of the most remarkable and indisputable laws in literature and art that those who are identified with nature and human nature, as it appears in their native country, are at the same time most cosmopolitan, still it is, after all, not so much in the subjects as in the treatment that the individnality of a national art is best demonstrated. It is when the artist is so thoroughly imbued with the spirit of the institutions of his native land that it appears in his art, whatever be the subject—it is then that he is most national. We hear a great deal about the French school and the English school; but it is not because each school finds its subjects invariably at home that it possesses an individuality of its own, but because we see unconsciously reflected in it the influences of the land that gave it birth. For this reason, if an English and a French painter shall each take the same scene, and that a wholly foreign one, say an Oriental group, although the subject be a foreign subject and identical in each canvas, you can discern at once that one picture is English, the other French in treatment. Each artist has stamped upon his work the impression of the influences of the people to which he belongs.

Patriotism, a wholesome enthusiasm for one's own country, seems, then, in some occult way to lie at the basis of a native art, and native art founded on knowledge is therefore always the truest art; while the artist who is thus inspired will generally find material enough to call forth his æsthetic yearnings and arouse his creative faculties at his own door.

SAIL-BOAT.—[WINSLOW HOMER.]

In passing from *genre* to our later portraiture we do not find the same proportionate activity and intelligent progress that we see in other departments of our art, although some creditable painters in this department can be mentioned. Harvey A. Young, of Boston, has shown a good eye for color, and seizes a likeness in a manner that is artistically satisfactory, while he does not so often grasp the character of the sitter as his external traits. Mr. Custer, of the same city, charmingly renders the infantile beauty of childhood, its merry blue eyes, the dimpled roses of the cheeks, and the flaxen curls that ripple around the shoulders. There is, however, too much sameness in his work—a too apparent tendency to mannerism. Mrs. Henry Peters Grey has a faculty of making a pleasing likeness. She has executed some portrait plaques in majolica that are remarkable evidences of the progress ceramic art is now making in the United States. Mrs. Loop is one of our successful portrait-painters. Her works are not strikingly original, but they are harmonious in tone and color, and poetical in treatment. Henry A. Loop has also executed some pleasing portraits and ideal compositions; of the latter, his "Echo" is perhaps the most successful rendering of female beauty he has attempted. George H. Story should be included among the most important portrait-painters of this period. His work is characterized by vigor of style and pleasing color; he seizes a likeness without any uncertainty in technique. His *genre* compositions and ideal heads are also inspired by a refined taste and correct perception of the principles of art. William Henry Furness, of Philadelphia, who died in 1867, just as he reached his prime, was allied in genius to the great masters of portraiture of the early stages of our art. He matured slowly. His first efforts showed only small promise; but he had the inestimable quality of growth, and has been equalled by few of our painters in the study and rendering of character. When he had a sitter he would give days to a preliminary and exhaustive study of his mental and moral traits.

In Darius Cobb, of Boston, great earnestness is apparent in the pursuit of art, together with an exalted opinion of what should be the aims of æsthetic culture. Mr. Cobb has attempted sculpture, monumental art, portraiture, and the painting of religious compositions. We consider it a promising sign to see an artist of such energy seeking to exalt the character of his pursuit. His works seem, however, to show the lack of a systematic course of training in the rudiments of technique; but in such strong and characteristic portraits as that of Rufus Choate he has exhibited decided ability.

The historic art of the period has been neither prolific nor attractive, with a few exceptions. The late war has given rise to some important works, like Winslow Homer's notable "Prisoners to the Front;" and Julian Scott has been measurably successful in such paintings as "In the

"THE SCOUT."—[WORDSWORTH THOMPSON.]

Cornfield at Antietam," representing a charge in that memorable battle, which belongs to a class of pictures of which we hope to have more in the future. There is a striving after originality in his paintings that is in the right direction. Mrs. C. A. Fassett, who has executed some excellent portraits, has also recently composed an important painting of the "Electoral Commission," of whose merits the writer can only speak by report.

In Wordsworth Thompson we find an artist who seems to realize the possibilities of American historical art. Although a pupil of Gleyre, and for a number of years a resident abroad, there is no evidence of servile subserviency to any favorite school or method in the style of Mr. Thompson. He is an excellent draughtsman, his color is a happy medium between the high and low keys of different schools—fresh, cool, and crisp—

"ON THE OLD SOD."—[WILLIAM MAGRATH.]

and his work is thoroughly finished, and yet broad in effect. He evidently has no hobbies to ride. As a designer of horses he has few equals in this country. If we have a fault to find with him, it is in a certain lack of snap, of warmth, of enthusiasm in the handling of a subject, which renders it less impressive than it might otherwise be.

Mr. Thompson, in his Mediterranean wanderings, gathered material for a number of attractive coast scenes, effective in atmosphere and in the

"A MATIN SONG."—[FIDELIA BRIDGES.]

rendering of figures, feluccas, and waves, all tending to illustrate his versatility. But he deserves to be most widely known on account of scenes taken from Southern life, and historic compositions suggested by the late war, or illustrating notable events of the Revolution. For pictures of this description Mr. Thompson seems to us to rank next to Trumbull, whose masterly paintings of the "Death of Montgomery" and the "Battle of

STUDY OF A DOG.—[FRANK ROGERS.]

Bunker Hill," now at New Haven, have hitherto been by far the most remarkable military paintings produced by an American artist. There is less action, fire, and brilliance of color in Mr. Thompson's works, but they possess many admirable qualities that entitle them to much respect. Among the most notable is an elaborate composition representing the Continental army defiling before General Washington and his staff at Philadelphia. The group of officers and horses in the foreground is one of the best pieces of artistic work recently painted by an American.

When we come to a consideration of animal painting in this period of our æsthetic culture, we find that it is the most barren of good results of any branch of our art. We are at a loss to account for this, especially as the evidences of promise are also less prominent than in landscape and genre. Not only has the number of the artists who have pursued this department been proportionately small, but the quality of their work has been of a low average, and lacking in the originality elsewhere apparent.

In the painting of pastoral scenes, with cattle, Peter Moran, of Philadelphia, probably shows the most originality and force; and Thomas Robinson, of Boston, has displayed exceptional vigor in painting the textures of cattle, but without much invention in composition. James Hart for the past twelve years has made a specialty of introducing groups of cattle into his idyllic landscapes. They are often well drawn and carefully painted, and are in general effect commendable, although, like most of our animal painters, Mr. Hart does not seem to have got at the character of the animal as Snyders, Morland, or Landseer would have done. Mr. Dolph has painted some creditable cats and pugs in combination with interiors; and two young artists, Messrs. George Inness, Jun., and J. Ogden Brown, have executed some promising cattle pieces.

Miss Bridges must be credited with developing a charming and original branch of art, of which thus far she seems to enjoy a monopoly. There is exquisite fancy, as well as capital art, in the method in which, with water-colors, she composes stalks of grain or wild-flowers in combination with field birds, meadow-larks, linnets, bobolinks, sparrows, or sand-pipers, balancing on the apex of a wavering stalk, or flying over the wheat or by the sands of the sea-beat shore.

Mr. Frank Rogers, who is still a very young man, takes especial interest in painting dogs, although not intending to confine himself to that branch of animal life, and has already achieved considerable success in his attempts to represent canine traits. He has trained several dogs to pose for him for ten to fifteen minutes at once. In the decided ability and success already shown by Mr. Rogers we can see that it is now possible for our artists, availing themselves of influences already at work here, combined with an intense love of nature and the ideal, to do strong original work without devoting half their lives to foreign study, and thus carry on to a higher stage the national art for which so many clamor unreasonably, not considering that new schools of art are not born in a day, nor evolved without the conditions which have invariably prepared the way for the national art of other people. Art travels by no royal road.

Our continent is not so plentifully stocked with wild beasts and game as some parts of the Old World, but we yet have the panther and the bison, although now fast fading into a mere traditionary existence before the rifle of the pioneer. R. M. Shurtleff has a pleasant fancy for catamounts and deer, and has been a careful student of their habits, of which the results appear in dramatic bits of the wild life of the woods introduced into effective paintings of forest scenery; "A Race for Life" is the title of a weird, savage, and powerful composition by this artist, representing a flock of ravening wolves pursuing their victim over fields of frozen snow, behind which the low red sun is setting; and A. F. Tait has also devoted his life to rescuing from oblivion species which are rapidly becoming extinct, unless our game-laws are better enforced than they have been hitherto. There is often too finished a touch to the style of Mr. Tait, which deprives it of the force it might otherwise have; but he has, on the other hand, painted both game and domestic animals with remarkable truth, and

"LOST IN THE SNOW."—[A. F. TAIT.]

he brings to the subject an inventive fancy that greatly adds to the variety and interest of his works. We might add in this connection an allusion to the ingenious carvings of Alexander Pope, a young artist who not only cuts out groups of game from a block of wood with much cleverness, but also truthfully colors the grouse and teal his skilful knife carves out of pine.

There is a branch of art which latterly has attracted much attention in this country. We refer to still-life. George H. Hall, who is also known as a *genre* painter, justly earned a reputation years ago for effective painting of fruit and flowers, in which he has hitherto had few equals in this country; and M. J. Heade has devoted his attention successfully to the rendering of the wonderful gorgeousness of tropical vegetation. The ideal flower-painting of Mr. Lafarge we have already mentioned. Miss Robbins, of Boston, is at present one of the most prominent artists we have in this department. She composes with great taste, and lays on her colors with superb effect. Some of her paintings suggest the rich, massive coloring of Van Huysams. Messrs. Seavey, of Boston, Way, of Baltimore, and Lambdin, of Philadelphia, have produced some interesting results in this direction; and Miss Dillon and Mrs. Henshaw must be credited with some very beautiful floral compositions. The list of ladies who have been measurably successful in realistic flower-painting is very large, and indicates the strong tendency toward decorative art in the country, which must result ere long in a distinctly national type of that branch of æsthetic culture.

In arriving at the close of the second period of American painting, we are encouraged by abundant evidences of a healthy activity. While some phases of our art, after a growth of half a century, are passing through a transition period, and new methods and theories are grafting themselves upon the old, there is everywhere apparent a deeper appreciation of the supreme importance of the ideal, and a gathering of forces for a new advance against the strongholds of the materialism that wars against the culture of the ideal, combined with a rapidly spreading consciousness on the part of the people of the ethical importance of art, and a disposition to co-operate in its healthful development. At the same time new influences are entering into the national culture of æsthetics, and branches which have hitherto received little attention from our artists are coming rapidly into prominence, suggesting that we are about entering upon a third stage of American art.

V.
SCULPTURE IN AMERICA.

IT is a generally conceded fact that since the death of Michael Angelo the art of sculpture has made little progress in the expression of the ideal. It has rather indicated, until recently, a lack of steadiness of purpose, and a want of freshness and intellectual grasp that place the plastic art of the last three centuries in a lower rank than that of the Classic and the Middle Ages. It is, therefore, a matter of surprise that in a people apparently so unideal as our own, and engaged in struggling to win for itself a right to exist among the wilds of a new world, that we find that so much evidence has already been shown of an appreciation for sculpture. It is true that we have not yet produced any masterpieces that can rank with those of antiquity; but, on the other hand, some of our plastic art compares favorably with the best that has been created in modern times.

But what might have been expected under the circumstances has proved to be the case. Originality has been the exception and not the rule, even with our best sculptors. Naturally led to study the antique in Europe, and also to master there the technical elements of the art of sculpture, owing to the entire absence of facilities for art education here, it was only to be expected that they would at first yield to the art influences whose guidance they sought. It was not their fault that, until recently, those influences were conventional, and based upon a false perception of the principles of art.

Some of our most successful sculptors have never been abroad, or at least have not systematically placed themselves under the tuition of a foreign master; while a number of them have indicated in their tendencies a natural sympathy with the later movement of modern sculpture, which is rather in the direction of allegory, portraiture, and *genre* suggested by domestic life. When the ancients represented Venus or Jove in marble, they sculptured a being in whose actual existence they believed, and thus a profound reverence inspired the work of the master. When the sculptor of the Middle Ages carved the deeds of the Saviour, or the saints, or represented the Last Judgment, he was moved by deep love or reverential awe, and an unquestioning belief in the events he was commemorating. But when the sculptor of this century undertakes to revive classical subjects and modes of thought, he encounters an insurmountable obstacle at the outset, which checks all progress, and relegates his art to a secondary rank, without even the benefit of a doubt in his favor. The laws and limitations of mind make it impossible for an art to be of the first order which depends upon the imitation of other art. It is only by copying nature directly, under the inspirations of its own age and country, that a school of art has the slightest chance of immortality. Thorwaldsen, the greatest sculptor since Michael Angelo, exemplified this truth to a remarkable degree. Moved by a realization of classic art which no other modern sculptor except Flaxman has approached, we yet find his classical subjects inferior to those allegorical subjects in which he gave expression to the impulses of his own times. A slowly dawning consciousness that art cannot by any force of will or free agency escape from these limitations of growth is becoming at last

"EVE BEFORE THE FALL."—[HIRAM POWERS.]

evident in recent sculpture, especially in the emotional and sometimes sensational sculpture of France. Lacking repose, it is yet fresh and original, and is destined by continued self-assertion to reach a high rank.

It is in imitations of the antique or in allegory, and portraiture, that our sculpture has exerted its best efforts, until within a few years. General Washington has also proved a sort of Jupiter Tonans to our sculptors. Elevated to a semi-apotheosis by the people, he has hitherto been the most prominent subject of the plastic art of the West, and has thus afforded a fair standard of comparison between the merits of different artists, since very few of them but have tried their hand with the national hero. As regards popular appreciation or pecuniary reward, it must be admitted that our sculptors have relatively little cause for complaint.

The art of sculpture was by no means unknown here when the white man first stepped foot on our shores. The pipe-stone quarries of the West are an evidence of what had already been attempted by the aboriginal savages. Tobacco, so much maligned by certain zealous philanthropists, was at least an innocent cause of some of the earliest attempts at sculpture made on this continent. The writer has in his possession an Indian pipe carved out of flint, which represents a man sitting with hands clasped across his knees. Simple as it is, it indicates good skill in stone-carving, and considerable observation of race characteristics and anatomy. Evidences of great technical skill in the plastic arts, but with an unformed perception of beauty, are being constantly discovered among the relics of the extinct Mound-builders of the West and South.

Before the Revolution, however, excepting in the carving of figureheads, plastic art, unlike painting, seems to have been hardly known in the United States. And so little sign was there of its dawn that John Trumbull declared to Frazee, as late as 1816, that sculpture "would not be wanted here for a century." But even then the careful observer might have noticed indications that a genius for glyptic art was awakening in the new republic. In the early part of the last century Deacon Drowne made a vane for Faneuil Hall, and one for the Province House, in Boston, which appear to have gained him great repute in his day in New England. The latter work, although turning with the wind on an iron spindle, was a life-size statue of an Indian sachem holding a bow and arrow in the act of aiming. It was hollow, and of copper, and would seem, from the impression it made, to have been a work of some merit. Somewhat later, Patience Wright, of Bordentown, New Jersey, displayed considerable cleverness in modelling miniature wax heads in relief, and by this process succeeded in making likenesses of Washington and Franklin, among the celebrities of her time. William Rush, who was born some twenty years before the Revolution, had also shown already that even in ship-carving the sculptor may find scope for fancy and skill, as Matthew Pratt, in the previous generation, had proved that even in the painting of signs genius can find vent for its inspirations. Rush was undoubtedly a man of genius; for, although all the art education he ever had was confined to an apprenticeship with a ship-carver, his figure-heads of Indians or naval heroes added a singular merit to the beauty of the merchant marine which

"ORPHEUS."—[THOMAS CRAWFORD.]

first carried our flag to the farthest seas, and the men-of-war that wrested victory in so many a hard-fought battle. Rush worked only in wood or clay; but original strength and talent, which under better circumstances might have achieved greater results, are evident in some of his portrait busts, and in a statue of a nymph at Fairmount. A bust of himself, carved out of a block of pine, is remarkable for a realistic force and character that entitle it to a permanent place in the records of American sculpture.

Sculpture, however, was much more backward in gaining a foothold in the country than the sister arts; for it was not until 1824 that the first portrait in marble by a native was executed—that of John Wells, by John Frazee, a stone-cutter, whose sole art education was obtained during an apprenticeship in a yard where rude monumental work was turned out for the bleak cemeteries in use before such sumptuous retreats as Greenwood and Mount Auburn were planned. There was a feeling after the ideal in the nature of this unassisted artist which enabled him to be potential in influencing younger artists; while his opportunities were unfavorable to the just development of his own abilities.

Rush began to model in clay in 1789, and at that time not one of the artists who have since given celebrity to our native sculpture had seen the light. Frazee was born in 1790; and Hezekiah Augur, of New Haven, in 1791. The latter was engaged in the grocery trade, and failing in that, took up modelling and wood-carving, without any guide except his natural instincts. Like many of our first sculptors, his efforts are interesting rather as evidences of what talent entirely uninstructed and untrained can accomplish, than for any intrinsic value in his work. Many of the artists who have succeeded him have also begun life in some trade or profession altogether at variance with the art to which they afterward consecrated their lives.

It was not till the year 1805, long after Copley, West, Malbone, Allston, and Stuart had demonstrated our capacity for pictorial art, that the genius of the country seemed inclined to allow us a plastic art of our own. In that year Hiram Powers was born, one of the best known sculptors of the century. The same year witnessed the birth of Horatio Greenough. In the remote wilds of Kentucky, still harried by the Indians, Hart was born in 1810; and Clevenger, Crawford, and Mills followed in 1812, 1813, and 1815—all artists of note, even if of unequal merits, and important as pioneers in the art rather than the creators of a great school of sculpture. Thus we see that without any apparent previous preparation a strong impulse toward glyptic art and the men to direct and give it strength simultaneously sprung up in the land. When one considers the disadvantages under which they labored, and that, so far as can be known, they were not even aided by any heredity of genius in this direction, criticism is tempered by surprise that they achieved the results they did, and that two of them at least—Powers and Crawford—succeeded in winning for themselves a European renown which made them almost the peers of some of the leading foreign sculptors of the age, who were born amidst the trophies of classic and Renaissance art.

"COLUMBUS BEFORE THE COUNCIL."—[FROM THE BRONZE DOOR OF THE CAPITOL AT WASHINGTON.—RANDOLPH ROGERS.]

Hiram Powers must always be assigned a commanding position in our Western art, even by those who are not enthusiastic admirers of his works. A farmer's boy of the Green Mountains, he early exchanged Vermont for the bustling streets of Cincinnati, where an ampler scope was offered to the aspiring energies of the founder of American sculpture. Like many of our sculptors, a turn for mechanics, characteristic of the inventive mind of the people, was combined in him with a capacity for art, and this, which at first found vent in a study of the inventions of the time, enabled him in maturer life to facilitate the means of art expression by valuable inventions. Palmer and several other American sculptors have also aided the art in a similar way. From modelling in wax, which aroused great local interest, young Powers proceeded to modelling in plaster, under the tuition of a German artist resident in Cincinnati, and, aided by the generous patronage of Mr. Longworth—to whose liberality toward our artists American art is greatly indebted—he soon received numerous commissions for portrait busts of some of our most notable public men, such as Webster, Jackson, Marshall, and Calhoun. Notwithstanding his lack of training and art associations, Powers executed some of these portraits with a vigor worthy of the subjects, and scarcely equalled by any of his subsequent work.

In 1837 Powers decided to go to Italy, whither Greenough had already preceded him, led thither, like many since, by superior art advantages and economical reasons, which still sway our sculptors at a time when it would seem that it would be more profitable, so far as native art is concerned, for them to remain here. Several of our sculptors have acknowledged to the writer that the time has come for their art to grow up under the home influences which are to regulate the art of the future, but that the question of economy forces them to live in Florence and Rome.

Residing in Florence until his death, Powers devoted his long career to the creation of many works of high finish, and occasionally of a merit comparing well with the works of an age whose plastic arts were conventional. Who has not seen the famous "Greek Slave," inspired by the enthusiasm for the Greeks struggling with the Turk for existence? The "Penseroso," "Fisher Boy," and "Proserpine" are also among the most pleasing works of this artist. The "California," a nude, symbolical female figure, is less satisfactory in conception, and is also open to criticism as to its proportions. In these works we see expressed the thoughts of an artist skilled in the technical requirements of the art, and moved by a lofty ideal, but marked by tender sentiment rather than force, and suggesting sometimes a dryness of style and a coldness or reticence of emotion inherited from the undemonstrative people of New England, as if when the artist was executing them the stern genius of Puritanism, jealous of the voluptuous or the passionate in art, had stood Mentor-like at his side and said, "There, that will do; beware lest your love of beauty lead you to forget that you are an American citizen, to whom duty, principle, example, are the watchwords of life." But sometimes genius proved superior to tradition even with Powers, as when he composed the two great ideal statues of Eve before and after the fall. By these noble works, inspired

"THE GHOST IN HAMLET."—[THOMAS R. GOULD.]

by true, untrammelled artistic feeling—which we must consider his best ideal compositions—he earned a rank very near to that of Gibson and Canova, and rendered his art worthy of lasting remembrance.

The art of Powers was best exemplified in his portrait busts. His imagination was not prolific or active, as one may infer from the following expressions of his own: "I could never satisfy myself with an ideal in a hurry. The human form is infinite. It is the image of God. I have found that, do my best, there was always a *better* in nature. Once knowing this, I have hesitated and sought to find it, and this is the way to fame.

One may fail with all his care and labor, but it is the only way. Not they who have produced the most, but they who have done the best, stand foremost in the end. I never felt that I had the power to charge a hundred statues. I exhaust myself on a few. This accounts for the fact that I found it necessary to give nearly a year's time, in all, to the model of your statue of 'Paradise Lost.'"

The early educational advantages of Horatio Greenough were superior to those of Powers; and as one of the first in our country to assert himself in marble, he won a name which we are reluctantly obliged to consider in excess of his merits as an artist. He impresses one as a man of intellectual force and culture, but without any special calling to sculpture. The work by which he will be known the longest is the Bunker Hill Monument, whose stately proportions he designed. Greenough executed a number of vigorous and striking busts, like those of Lafayette and Fenimore Cooper, which deserve favorable mention. But in venturing after ideal expression he cannot be said to have accomplished satisfactory results. The elaborate group called "The Rescue," on the portico of the Capitol at Washington, is ambitious, but leaves one to regret that so prominent a position could not have been more appropriately decorated.

Few statues have ever given rise to more conflicting criticisms than Greenough's "Washington" in the grounds of the Capitol. Colossal in size and on a massive throne, seated half nude and holding out a Roman sword in his left hand, some one has jocularly observed that the august hero of the republic seems to say, "Here is my sword; my clothes are in the Patent-office yonder." It certainly seems an absurdity in this age to represent so recent a character in a garb in which he was so rarely seen by the public, or so closely and incongruously to imitate the style of the antique. Benjamin West showed more originality and courage when, in the last century, and in defiance of the opinion of such men as Sir Joshua Reynolds, he dared to break loose from the conventional, and created a revolution in historical art by permitting General Wolfe to die in the clothes in which he went to battle. But in justice to Greenough, whose statue is in some respects meritorious and important, especially in the bass-reliefs on the elegant chair, it should be said that he never designed to have this statue placed in its present position, but under the dome of the Rotunda, where it would undoubtedly be far more impressive, and being sheltered from the winter snows, its nudity would be less incongruous.

GEORGE WASHINGTON.—[J. Q. A. WARD.]

Last year a sculptor died at Florence who was born in Kentucky nearly seventy years ago. His education was confined to three months in a district school, and his first occupation was chimney-building. James Hart, although successful in portraiture, was also an idealist, who, after settling in Italy, produced numerous pleasing works, like his "Angelina" and "Woman Triumphant." There is a delicate, winning sense of beauty and a refined emotional tendency in his art, which pleases while it fails to master us, because it was a facile fancy rather than a lofty imagination that conceived his creations.

Shobal V. Clevenger, a stone-cutter of Ohio, presents another instance of the sudden yearning toward the plastic art which early in the century sought vent in various parts of the country. Like so many others, he turned his face to Italy to find the knowledge which it was impossible for his native land to give him at that time. The nation owes a debt of gratitude to him, as to several of our early sculptors, for many truthfully realistic portraits of our leading statesmen and poets.

In point of date as well as in ability we find that Thomas Crawford, a native of New York State, was one of the first of our sculptors. If Powers was remarkable for the refinement of his work, in the sculpture of Crawford we find a certain grandiose style not too common in our art, and at the same time so harmoniously rendered as to avoid exaggeration. Crawford occupies among our sculptors a position corresponding to that of Allston among our early painters. There is a classic majesty about his works, a sustained grandeur that is warmed by a sympathetic nature, and brought within the range of the throes and aspirations of this tumultuous century. He had what most of our sculptors have lacked—genius. Were he alive to-day, when a new order of sculpture is bursting its bonds, he would have few peers. Among his most important works are the impressive equestrian statue of Washington at Richmond, and the colossal statue of Beethoven in the Music Hall at Boston. They were cast in the foundries of Müller at Munich, and were hailed by all, artists and sovereign alike, with a dramatic enthusiasm which speaks eloquently for the estimate placed upon them in one of the most notable art tribunals of Europe.

The bronze door of the Capitol at Washington, containing panel groups illustrative of the American Revolution, has been considered by some to be a masterpiece of Crawford, and it certainly indicates imagination and technical skill unusual among us until recently; but the statue of Orpheus descending into Tartarus in search of his wife Eurydice seems, on the whole, to be the most symmetrical and just representative work of this great sculptor. His stately and graceful statue of "Liberty" on the dome of the Capitol is also entitled to high consideration, but one can hardly think of it without indignation, for certainly nothing was ever devised quite so absurd as to create a work of imagination like this, and then to perch it up in the air three hundred feet above the ground, where it is a mere shapeless spot against the sky, its beauty almost as completely snatched away from human ken as if it were buried as far beneath the surface of the earth.

The art of the Capitol at Washington presents, indeed, a most extraordinary farrago of excellence and eccentricity and ignorance. Some of the alto-relievos in the Rotunda are of such exceptional uncouthness that one is astounded to think that some of the men are still living who permitted them to be placed there. They might easily be passed off for rude Aztec relics. The Sculpture Hall adjoining displays the same amazing incongruity. Its existence suggests a dim perception in the builders that at some future time we should need a national gallery of statuary; while the inequality in the merit of the sculptures already placed there would indicate that they had been chosen entirely by lot rather than by deliberate selection. Not until a permanent national art commission like that of France is appointed can we hope, in the present unæsthetic condition of Congress, to have such art collected at the national capital as will be entirely creditable to the country. Such a commission, owing to the frailty

"MEDEA."—[WILLIAM WETMORE STORY.]

"THE PROMISED LAND."—[FRANKLIN SIMMONS.]

of human nature, might perhaps show partiality at times toward a favorite-school; but what it did admit would at least be of a higher average merit, and mere tyros in art would have no chance to storm the public Treasury by the sheer force of lobbying.

It is to the then absolute ignorance of art on the part of the people that we owe the equestrian statues of Clark Mills — a contemporary of Crawford — of which the most noted is probably the statue of General Jackson opposite the White House, and the one of George Washington, for which he received $50,000. The former is chiefly notable for the mechanical dexterity which so balanced the weights that the prancing steed is actually able to stand in that position without other support than its own ponderosity. That Mr. Mills has ability is unquestioned, for it is said that before ever he had seen a statue he was able to take a portrait bust of Calhoun which is pronounced a striking likeness; but it is dexterity and talent rather than genius which he possesses. There is little evidence of art feeling in his works, and the prominence that has been given to them is a just cause of regret to the lover of art.

It is pleasant among so much poor art to find here and there works like those of Crawford, Ward, Brown, Randolph Rogers, and Ball, which indicate an earnest striving after a lofty art ideal. Henry K. Browne, one of our earliest sculptors, will probably be best known by his two equestrian statues—of General Washington, in Union Square, New York, and General Scott, at the capital. It is extremely difficult to tell what it is which makes such monuments so rarely satisfactory. If the horse is anatomically correct, it is, perhaps, ungraceful; or if pleasing in that respect, then the horse-fancier comes along, who tells you that it cannot be justly admired, for it is incorrect in the details. Between these two objections one is often at a loss to give an opinion; and in point of fact the famous statue of Colleoni by Verrochio, made in the Middle Ages, seems thus far to be almost the only wholly acceptable equestrian work since the classic times, so thoroughly does it seem in its firm, massive, yet energetic lines to embody the description of the war-horse given in the Book of Job, and so nobly does his mailed rider bestride him. The cause of the difficulty appears to be the same as in marine painting. To paint a ship one should love it intensely, and if he does, he is likely to comprehend the action; to design a horse in motion one should love horses, and in such case the study of them begins instinctively in childhood. But most sculptors have no

"LATONA AND HER INFANTS."—[W. H. RINEHART.]

natural equine bias, and, after accepting a commission for an equestrian statue, they begin to study the horse for the purpose of information, rather than from sympathetic, enthusiastic feeling.

Mr. Browne has struggled with these difficulties with very creditable success. Neither of the statues mentioned above gives complete satisfaction, but they are doubtless among the best yet exhibited in our country. That of Scott represents the finest horse, and very graceful and interesting it is, although the proportions are rather those of an Arab steed than of an American war-horse; while that of Washington is the most spirited and attractive. It is heroic and impressive in its general effect. This artist, who still resides at Newburgh, enjoying a green old age after a successful career, has accomplished much ideal work, like the pleasing statue of "Ruth," and has shown a fine artistic feeling in his conceptions, although hardly entitled to a foremost rank in this branch of the art.

Thomas Ball, who was originally a portrait-painter, and who continues to adorn our public squares with meritorious sculptures, is another artist to whom we are indebted for one of the most spirited and correct equestrian statues in the country. We refer to his "Washington," in the Public Garden in Boston. Pleasing when regarded artistically, cavalrymen also like it for its truth to nature. The group called "Emancipation," in Lincoln Park, at Washington, is also by Mr. Ball.

An equestrian statue that is destined to occupy a high position in our native art is that of General Thomas, by J. Q. A. Ward. It is of colossal size, and has been cast in bronze at Philadelphia. There is a force in the action, an originality in the pose, a justness in the proportions of both horse and rider, that render it exceptionally excellent. In Mr. Ward we see one of the most vigorous and individual sculptors of the age. As an influence in our art his example is of great importance, because while placing at its true value the good that may be obtained by familiarity with the models of classic art, whether by the study of casts at home or abroad, he recognizes the basal principle of all true art—that its originating force must proceed from within, and that culture can only supplement, but cannot supply the want of, genius in the artist or the people. And thus, while thoroughly conversant with foreign and antique art, Mr. Ward has worked at home, and drawn the sources of his inspiration from native influences. He has a mind overflowing with resources; his fancy is never still; he is ever delighting to sketch in clay, if the term may be so used. Many are familiar with the noble statue of Shakspeare and the "Indian Hunter" in the Central Park. The latter, although not in all respects anatomically correct, is in spirit and design one of the most notable works produced by American plastic art. But the bronze statue of Washington recently set up at Newburyport is, perhaps, the best existing specimen of Mr. Ward's skill. The subject is not a new one; in fact, it has been treated so many hundred times in one form or another that especial originality was needed to render it again with any degree of freshness and interest. But the effort has been crowned with success. There is in this statue, which is of colossal size, a sustained majesty, dignity, and repose, and a harmony of design rarely attained in modern sculpture.

Among the foremost of American sculptors in point of native ability we must accord a place to Benjamin Paul Akers, of Portland. He was indeed a man of genius, of a finely organized temperament; but he died before the maturity of his powers, ere he was able to achieve little more than a promise of immortality. His "Pearl Diver," which is indeed an exquisite creation, original, and tenderly beautiful, represents a youth whose corpse the tide has washed on the rocks, where it lies wrapped by the sea-weed, and tranquil in the repose of death. The anatomy and composition of this work are evidently the offspring of a finely-organized mind well grounded in the principles of his art, and inspired by tender sympathies and a strongly creative imagination; and his "St. Elizabeth" is also a lovely piece of sculpture. The noble ideal bust of Milton, and the "Pearl Diver," are grandly described by Hawthorne in the "Marble Faun." The admirable description of Kenyon, the young sculptor mentioned in that weird romance, is intended for a likeness of Akers.

"ZENOBIA."—[HARRIET HOSMER.]

Edward S. Bartholomew, of Connecticut, who died in his thirty-sixth year, was another of our most gifted sculptors. There was an affluence of fancy in his art, rare in our sculpture, which needed pruning rather than urging by foreign study. Naturally his works are unequal in merit; but the "Eve Repentant," "Ganymede," and "Hagar and Ishmael" will long perpetuate his fame. It is a noteworthy circumstance that Bartholomew was totally color-blind. This, in the opinion of many, is no disqualification in a sculptor; but some sculptors not only think otherwise, but are also conscious of a sense of color when creating a work.

Italy, which has been the home and second mother to most of the artists we have named, has long given a home to and inspired the art of a number of our most prominent sculptors, who are now permanently residing in Florence and Rome—Randolph Rogers, Story, Rinehart, Meade, Gould, Thompson, Miss Hosmer, and several others, all of whom merit more than a passing notice. Rogers, who has executed many exquisite works indicating fine sentiment and fancy, is most favorably known for the bronze doors in the Rotunda of the Capitol at Washington. Eight panels, representing scenes in the history of Columbus, have afforded abundant scope for the exhibition of a genius which, while it borrowed the idea from Ghiberti, had yet ability sufficient to give us an original work. The "Angel of the Resurrection," for the monument of Colonel Colt at Hartford, is also an important and beautiful creation by this artist. Larkin J. Meade, of Vermont, has justly won a wide reputation for portrait and monumental works, like that to Abraham Lincoln at Springfield, Illinois. It is of colossal dimensions, costing nearly $300,000, and in size and importance ranks with the majestic monument at Plymouth

"EVENING."—[E. D. PALMER.]

designed by Hammatt Billings. One of the noblest art opportunities of the century was offered when that monument was proposed. If Mr. Billings's original design had been fully carried out a work would have been erected of which the country might justly be proud. Lack of funds and a pitiful lack of enthusiasm resulted in reducing the dimensions of the work by half. Martin Milmore has also executed some very important civic monuments, and has turned the late war to account by numerous military memorials erected to our dead heroes. The one recently finished at Boston is the most noteworthy. The art represented in these works is, however, not of a high order, perhaps because such subjects are so trite that even an artist of very unusual ability would be staggered in treating them. Franklin Simmons, whose abilities have been chiefly devoted to a similar class of works with those of Meade and Milmore, often exhibits true art feeling, and a sense of the beautiful that makes his art exceptionally attractive. The monument to the Army and Navy, at Washington, which he has designed, is not wholly satisfactory, but it contains some effective points. One of his best works is the statue of Roger Williams. Another Americo-Florentine artist who has created some remarkable and beautiful ideal works is Thomas R. Gould. Among these may be mentioned "The Ascending Spirit," at Mount Auburn, "The Ghost in *Hamlet*," and "The West Wind." The latter is fascinating rather for the delicate fancy it shows than for technic knowledge, for it is open to criticism in the details; the drapery, for example, is so full as to draw away the attention from the figure. This is a blemish quite too common even in our best sculpture. Mr. Gould has also been very successful in portraiture, and is now engaged on a full-sized statue of Kamehameha, late King of the Sandwich Islands. In the ideals of this artist we notice a powerful originality, and an attempt to render in marble effects usually left to the higher orders of pictorial art. Allegory he treats with marked power, and such ideal conceptions as the heads of Christ and of Satan suggest possibilities scarcely yet touched by sculpture.

Another of our sculptors, working near the quarries whence comes the marble into which he stamps immortality, was W. H. Rinehart, of Baltimore, one of the truest idealists whom this country has produced. Criticism is almost disarmed as one gazes at his "Sleeping Babes," or the tender grace of "Latona and her Infants."

In all these artists we find more or less dexterity of execution and delicacy of sentiment, but are rarely impressed by a sense that any of them indicate great reserve force. In William W. Story this idea is more clearly conveyed. No American in the art world now occupies a more prominent position or shows greater versatility. Possessed of an ample fortune, and originally a lawyer, and preparing legal tomes, he then devoted himself to poetry, the drama, and general literature, and has succeeded as a sculptor to a degree which has caused a leading London journal to call him the first sculptor of the Anglo-Saxon race since the death of Gibson. He certainly occupies a commanding place, fairly won, among the

BUST OF WILLIAM PAGE.—[WILLIAM R. O'DONOVAN.]

prominent men of the age. But here our praise must be qualified; for it may be seriously questioned whether we are not dazzled by the sum of his abilities rather than by any exceptional originality and daring in anything Story has done. Of his sculpture it may be said that it indicates the work of a rich and highly cultivated mind; it is thoughtful, thoroughly finished, and classically severe. But it commands our respect rather than our enthusiasm. There is in it nothing inspirational. It is talent, not genius, which wrought those carefully executed marbles—talent of a high order, it is true. "Jerusalem Lamenting," "The Sibyl," and "Cleopatra" and "Medea," are works so noble, especially the first, that one is impatient with himself because he can gaze upon them so unmoved. The "Salome" is, perhaps, the most perfect work of this sculptor, who might have done greater things if he had not depended so exclusively upon foreign inspiration.

Miss Hosmer, who has resided in Italy ever since she took up art, has achieved a fame scarcely less than that of Mr. Story. This has doubtless been owing in part to her sex, for from the time of Sabina Von Steinbach until this century it has been exceedingly rare to see a woman modelling clay. But Miss Hosmer has a strong personality, and if her creations are not always thoroughly successful as works of art, they bear the vigorous impress of individual thought and imagination. She is best known in such versatile works as "Puck," "The Sleeping Sentinel," "The Sleeping Faun," and "Zenobia," in whose majestic proportions the artist has sought to express her ideal of a woman and a queen. Miss Hosmer took her first lessons in sculpture with Peter Stephenson, an artist who died too early to achieve a national reputation, although not too soon to be esteemed by his fellow-artists for his abilities. He studied awhile at Rome, and left a number of portrait busts, and a group of "Una and the Lion," which indicate undoubted talent. Other ladies who have essayed sculpture with success are Miss Stebbins, the biographer of Charlotte Cushman, and Mrs. Freeman, of Philadelphia, who has executed some beautiful works. Miss Whitney, who studied abroad for a time, but has wisely concluded to continue her work in this country, has shown a careful, thoughtful study of the figure, and is moved by a lofty idea of the position of sculpture among the arts. Among her more important works is an impressive statue of "Rome," in her decadence, mourning over her past glory; a statue of "Africa;" and one of Samuel Adams, in the Capitol at Washington.

There are other American sculptors deserving more than mere allusion, like Dexter, Richard Greenough, Barbee, Volk, Edmonia Lewis, Van Wart, Ives, Macdonald, Kernys, Ezekiel, Calverly, and Haseltine, who in portraiture or the ideal have won a more than respectable position; but our space limits us to a notice of several artists who, like Ward, combine great natural ability with traits distinctively American. One of these is Erastus D.

Palmer, of Albany, who has won transatlantic fame by the purity and originality of his art. The son of a farmer, and exercising the calling of a carpenter until nearly thirty, Palmer did not yield to the artistic yearnings of his nature until comparatively late in life. When he at last took up the pursuit of art, it was in his own town that he studied and sought fame, and his success was rapid and entirely deserved. Few of our sculptors have been such true votaries of the ideal, few have been able better

ABRAHAM PIERSON.—[LAUNT THOMPSON.]

to give it expression, and none have shown a type of beauty so national, or have more truly interpreted with an exquisite poetic sense the distinctive domestic refinement or religious thought of our people. It is beauty rather than power that we see expressed in the works of this true poet—

moral beauty identified with a type of physical grace wholly native. It is an art which finds immediate response here, for it is of our age and our land. Among the notable works of Palmer are his "Indian Captive,"

"THE CHARITY PATIENT."—[JOHN ROGERS.]

"Spring," "The White Slave," and "The Angel of the Sepulchre;" but we prefer to these the exquisitely beautiful bass-reliefs in which he has embodied with extreme felicity the domestic sentiments or the yearnings and aspirations of the Christian soul. The radical fault of Palmer's art is that he has depended more on his fancy than upon a direct study of nature for his compositions. The natural result has been that he soon began to lapse into mannerism, which has become more and more prominent in his later works.

Another sculptor of great ability owes his first instruction in the plastic art to Palmer — Launt Thompson. He was a poor lad who early showed art instincts, but was employed in the office of Dr. Armsby, until Palmer stated one day that he was in search of an assistant, and asked Dr. Armsby if he could recommend any one. The doctor suggested Thompson (who was in the room) as a youth who had a turn that way, but had been unable to find opportunity to gratify his art cravings. Thus began the career of one of our strongest portrait sculptors. In the modelling both of the bust and the full figure, Thompson has been equalled by very few American sculptors. Among many successful works may be mentioned his Napoleon, Edwin Booth, General Sedgwick, at West Point, and President Pierson, at Yale College. It is a cause for just regret that, after having achieved such success at home, Thompson should have deemed it necessary to take up his residence permanently in Italy.

Another artist whose work is entirely native to the soil is John Rogers, whose numerous statuette groups in clay have made him more widely known in the country than any other of our sculptors. A native of Salem, Massachusetts, and for awhile engaged in mechanical pursuits, this artist was at last able to turn his attention to plastic art,

"THE WHIRLWIND."—[J. S. HARTLEY.]

and went to Europe, where he seems to have gained suggestions from the realistic and impressional school of the later French sculptors; but this was rather as a suggestion than an influence, and, finding his mind

"ADORATION OF THE CROSS BY ANGELS." ST. THOMAS'S CHURCH, NEW YORK. —[ST. GAUDENS.]

more in sympathy with home life, he soon returned, and has ever since worked here, and from subjects of homely every-day *genre* around him. The late war has also furnished Rogers with material for many interesting groups. The art of Rogers is to the last degree unconventional, and in no sense appertains to what is called high art, but it springs from a nature moved by correct impulses, beating in unison with the time, and occupying the position of pioneer in the art of the future, because he has been true to himself and his age.

Daniel C. French, a pupil of Ward and Ball, is a young sculptor who, like Rogers, finds inspiration for his ideals in his native land, and gives promise of holding a prominent position in the field of American sculpture. He made a sudden and early strike for fame when, with scarce any instruction, he modelled the spirited and original, although anatomically imperfect, statue called the "Minute Man," which is at Concord.

Another strong representative of the new realistic school of sculpture that is gradually springing up in the community is W. R. O'Donovan, of Richmond, Virginia. Fighting sturdily on the side of the South during the late war, he as earnestly gives himself now to the pursuit of the arts of peace. He is not a rapid worker, but handles the clay with thoughtful mastery, and the results are stamped with the freshness and individuality of genius. Mr. O'Donovan's efforts have been most successful in portraiture, of which a striking example is given in the bronze bust of Mr. Page, the artist. Another bust, of a young boy, is as full of *naïve* beauty and refined sentiment and character as this is vigorous and almost startling in its grasp of individual traits.

The transition stage through which our plastic art is passing is also indicated by the stirring, realistic, and sometimes sensational art of a number of earnest and original young sculptors who have studied abroad, but have wisely concluded to return home, and to found, and grow up with, a new and progressive school of sculpture. One of these was the late Frank Dengler, of Cincinnati, who had studied at Munich, and was professor of sculpture at Boston; and others are Olin M. Warner, of New York, and Howard Roberts, of Philadelphia, who made the singularly bold statues of "Hypatia" and "Lot's Wife." To these may be added J. S. Hartley, who was recently Professor of Anatomy at the Art Students' League, and is now president of that flourishing institution. He began his career in Palmer's studio, and afterward studied in London and Paris. The art of these young sculptors is still immature and highly emotional or lyrical, and often verges on the picturesque rather than the severely classic. But if it lacks repose, on the other hand it is imaginative and powerful; its faults are

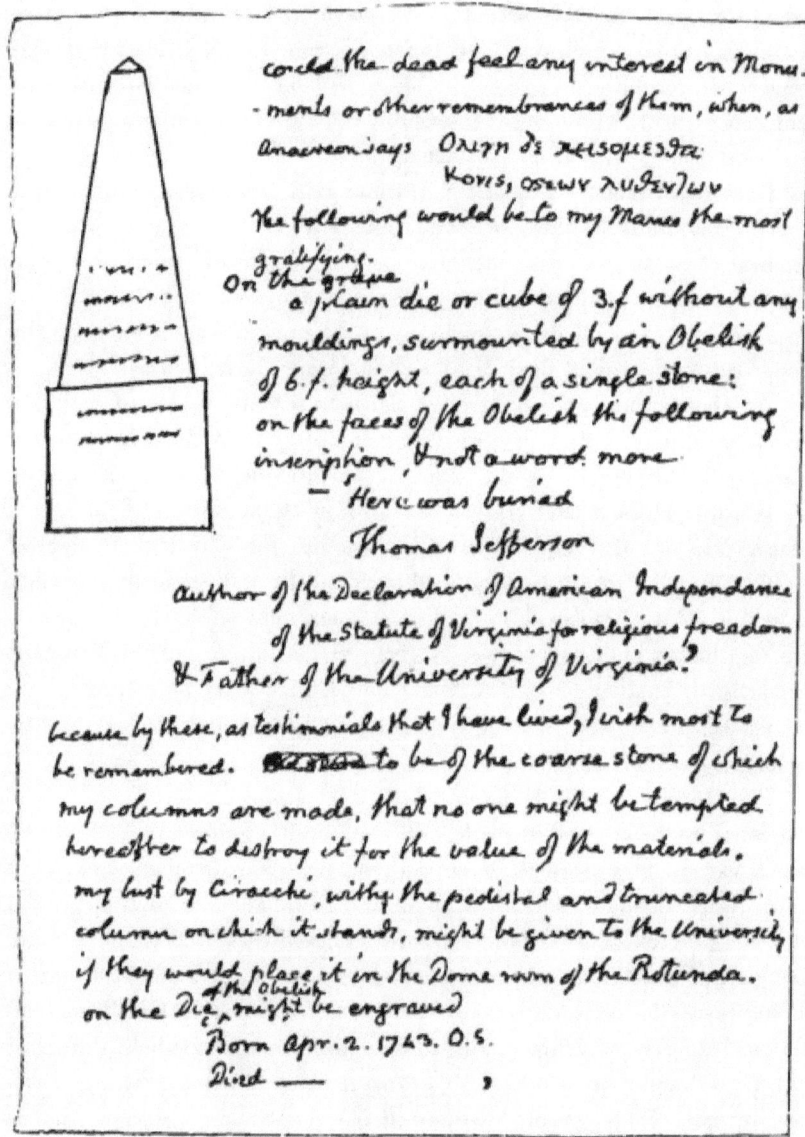

THOMAS JEFFERSON'S IDEA OF A MONUMENT.

those of an exuberant fancy that teems with thought; and these artists are undoubtedly the forerunners, if not the creators, of a thoroughly national school of sculpture. Superior in technic skill, moved by a genius thoroughly trained in the best modern school of plastic art, that of Paris, St. Gaudens, a native of New York, has given us, in the exquisite groups called "The Adoration of the Cross by Angels," in St. Thomas's Church, New York, one of the most important and beautiful works in the country. The Astor Reredos behind the altar at Trinity Church, designed by Mr. Withers, and partly executed here, is also a very rich addition to our plastic art, and is another sign that it is taking a direction little followed heretofore on this side the Atlantic. Dr. William Rimmer, who has recently died, powerful in modelling, a master of art anatomy, and author of a valuable work on that subject, also exerted an important influence in directing the studies of our rising sculptors. Having little sense of beauty, he understood art anatomy profoundly, and modelled with energy if not with grace. His statue of "The Gladiator" aroused astonishment in Paris: for as it is impossible for a living man to keep a falling position long enough for a cast to be taken, this masterly composition was necessarily a creation of the imagination based upon exhaustive knowledge of the figure.

Wood and stone carving and monumental work, and the decoration of churches and civic structures, have rarely been satisfactorily attempted here until recently. A curious paper and design left by Thomas Jefferson, of which we give a reduced fac-simile, is one of the earliest attempts at original monumental art in the United States. Here and there one of our sculptors has executed some good work in this field, but costly monuments have too often been erected in the country without much pretension to art. The increasing attention given to wood and stone carving, as in the new Music Hall at Cincinnati, the State Capitols at Albany and Hartford, and in some of our later churches, is a favorable sign that a broader field is opening at last for the fitting utterance of the rising genius of sculpture; while the numerous schools for instruction in this art that have been founded within the last decade, and the well-stored galleries of casts of the masterpieces of antiquity, are increasing the facilities for the growth of a home art. Enough has been said in this brief sketch to show that sculpture, if one of the latest of the arts to demand expression in the United States, has yet found a congenial soil in the New World.

VI.

PRESENT TENDENCIES OF AMERICAN ART.

AT the close of the fourth chapter of this volume it was briefly stated that new influences and forms of art expression have recently become prominent in our art, and are rapidly asserting their growing importance. With perhaps one or two exceptions, these new influences so gradually shade out of our former art that it is difficult to tell the exact moment when they assume an individuality of their own, and appear as new and distinct factors in the æsthetic culture of our people.

It is only when we take a retrospect of the whole field, and compare one generation with another, that we discern the vanishing point of one set of influences and the genesis of new schools, with the introduction of new branches of art culture in the community. Considering the progress of American art from this point of view, we find it divided most decidedly into periods, advancing with regular pace from one phase to another like the tints of a rainbow, shading off at the edges, but gradually becoming more intense. Thus we are able to trace in geometrical ratio the progress from primitive silhouettes and rude carvings up to the present comparatively advanced condition of the arts in this country.

And yet a closer inspection into the history of American art enables us to detect in its growth the same rapid spasmodic action, when once a start is made in a certain direction, as in other traits of our national development. There is a tropical vivacity in the manner in which with us bloom and fruition suddenly burst forth after a period of apparently unpromising barrenness. Thus West and Copley appeared almost fullfledged in art genius and capacity to adapt themselves to occupy prominent positions in Europe, and yet there were but few premonitory signs to indicate that the country was prepared for the advent of such artists.

Until recently, also, owing to some cause yet unsolved, we have not

"THE MOWING."—ALFRED FREDERICKS.

seemed able to develop more than one or two forms of art at once. At one period it was historic painting and portraiture; then portraiture, including for a time very marked success in miniature painting, headed by Fraser and Malbone, and continued by such able artists as T. S. Cummings, J. H. Brown, Miss Goodrich, and Mrs. Hall; then, all at once, landscape-painting made its appearance, and almost at a bound reached a good degree of merit. Hand in hand with landscape art came remarkable facility in line engraving. How rapidly excellence in this art was achieved in this country may be judged from the fact that in 1788 the editor of the *American Magazine* said apologetically, in presenting an incredibly rude plate of a dredging-machine in the magazine, "The editor has given the plate of the new machine for clearing docks, etc., because he had promised it. The want of elegant plates in a work of this kind is extremely regretted, and will, if possible, be supplied. If it cannot, the editor flatters himself that the infancy of the arts in America will be accepted as an apology for the defect." And yet not twenty years from that time Peter Maverick was doing good steel-engraving in New York; and scarce ten years later Durand was executing the masterly engravings of Trumbull's "Declaration of Independence" and Vanderlyn's "Ariadne." And from that time until recently engravers like James Smillie, senior, A. H. Ritchie, and John Marshall have carried this art to a high degree of excellence; while John Sartain has attained celebrity in mezzotint.

Strange as it may seem, while portraiture, landscape, and steel engraving were pursued with such success by our artists, a feeling for the other arts could hardly be said to exist. A sympathy with form, generally the earliest art instinct to show itself, was long in awakening, as proved by the tardiness of the plastic arts to demand expression among us; while to the resources of black and white, or *camieu*, or a perception of the matchless mystery and suggestiveness of *chiaro-oscuro*, the people have, until within a very short time, seemed altogether blind. Water-colors, also, were almost hooted at; wood-engraving was for long in a pitiful condition; and as for architecture and the decorative arts, nothing worthy of the name, and scarcely a sign of a perception of their meaning, could be said to exist on this side of the Atlantic.

Some years ago W. J. Linton, one of the most distinguished wood-engravers of the century, came to this country to live. Whether that had anything to do with the very rapid development of wood-engraving here since that time cannot be stated with certainty; but, judging from analogy, we should say that he has exerted a marked influence in stimulating the remarkable progress already reached by our engravers within a very few years. A. V. S. Anthony was one of the first to respond to the awakening demand for good wood-engraving here, and has shown great delicacy and skill in interpreting the drawings of our very clever artists in black and white. Charles Marsh is also an engraver of remarkable character and originality of style. In the rendering of a decorative or highly ideal class of subjects he brings to his aid an artistic genius not surpassed by any engraver we have produced. Messrs. Morse, Davis, Hoskin, Wolf, Annin, Juengling, Kingsley, Müller, Cole, Smithwick and French, Kreul, Dana, Andrew, and King, among a number who have distinguished themselves in this art, are especially noteworthy, not only for correct rendering of the spirit of a drawing, but often for individuality of style.

One of the most interesting phases of the development of wood-engraving in this country has been the discussion as to its position among the arts, and the merits of the recent method of engraving drawings or paintings photographed directly on the wood. This discussion has been interesting and valuable as another evidence of the activity and importance which the art question has already assumed in the community. That engraving is an art, one would think could never be disputed, if the question had not already been raised with a certain degree of acrimony on the part—strange as it may seem—of those who are often dependent upon the genius of the engraver for the recognition of their abilities by the public—the artists themselves. It seems to us to be sufficient answer to those who consider it purely a mechanical pursuit, that the simple fact that the higher the artistic perceptions of the engraver the better is the engraving he does, proves it to be a work of art.

On the other hand, it appears that the engraver may in turn assume too much when he claims to improve upon an illustration, or objects *per se* to cutting photographs on wood. While granting to engraving the rank of art, it cannot justly be forgotten that it is, after all, a means to an end, —an art, it is true, but an art subordinate to other arts which it is designed to interpret. Once this is allowed, it follows, as a matter of course, that it is the duty of the engraver to render faithfully the drawing or painting that is to be cut; and to magnify himself not at the expense of the artist who made the drawing, but by rendering, as nearly as possible,

a fac-simile of the original picture. If this be granted, then is it not clear that, instead of opposing, he should hail with satisfaction any new process which enables him to give on wood or any other material a closer copy of the style and spirit of the artist whom he is interpreting. That this can be done by a clever engraver by photographing a pen-and-ink drawing or painting directly on the wood, and then studying also the original work as he cuts it, seems to be no longer

"BIRDS IN THE FOREST."—[MISS JESSIE CURTIS.]

an open question. It has been demonstrated by too many excellent engravers within the last five years.

Another advantage of what we cannot but consider an advance in this art is, that it admits of a larger variety of styles, and a freer expression of the designer's methods of thought and feeling, and also enables many who do not care to work in the cramped limits of a block of wood to make a large composition in black and white, whether with Indian-ink or monochrome in oil, which is then photographed on the wood. In this way far greater freedom and individuality of handling is obtained, and a nobler utterance of the truths of nature. Can there be any question that a process which allows of such variety of expression must inure to art progress, and still more to the instruction of the people, who are directly benefited by the illustrations which are brought to their own doors, and placed in the hands of the young at the time when their tastes and characters are forming, and their imagination is most plastic and impressionable?

It would seem as if the art of wood-engraving had received in the most direct manner the action of some unseen hand, impelling it suddenly forward in this country by concerted action with the genius of illustration; for apparently by secret agreement that branch of art has within the last decade developed a comparative excellence yet reached by none of the sister arts in the land. And this turn for illustration has naturally been accompanied by an active movement in black and white drawing, particularly in crayon.

Samuel W. Rowse was one of the first to give an impetus to crayon drawing by a style of portraiture especially his own. As such he ranks with our leading portrait-painters; while the fact that he employed crayon as a medium for a time gave him a position almost entirely alone in this country. There is a wonderful subtlety in his power of seizing character and the rendition of soul in the faces he portrays. Equally happy in all the subjects he treats, he will be longest remembered, perhaps, for the many beautiful children's portraits he has executed. The success of Rowse naturally led to similar attempts by other artists; and in all our leading cities one may now find crayon artists who are more or less successful in the department of portraiture, among whom may be mentioned B. C. Munzig and Frederick W. Wright. Out of this has grown a school of landscape-artists employing charcoal—a medium that Lalanne and Allongé had already used with magical results. John R. Key, who is well known as a painter in oil, has, however, done his best work, as it seems to us, in charcoal. There is great tenderness in his treatment of light and shade, together with harmonious composition. J. Hopkinson Smith, known as a water-colorist, also handles charcoal like a master. He seizes his effects with the rapidity of improvisation, treats them in masses, and shows a feeling for *chiaroscuro* that is almost unique in our art.

When we come to the book illustrators we encounter a number of artists of merit, and occasionally of genius, who are so numerous that we can select only here and there a few of the most prominent names. Felix O. C. Darley was one of the first to show the latent capacity of our art in this branch. His style soon became

Representing the manner of PETER'S COURTSHIP.

[HOWARD PYLE.]

very mannered, but, at the same time, undoubtedly showed great originality and invention in seizing striking characteristics of our civilization, and a refined fancy in representing both humor and pathos. His linear illustrations to "Rip Van Winkle" and Judd's "Margaret" placed him, until recently, among our first two or three *genre* artists. Less versatile and inventive, Augustus Hoppin has, however, earned an honorable position among our earlier illustrators. Louis Stephens also won distinction for an elegant rendering of humorous subjects. Then followed a group of landscape illustrators, among whom Harry Fenn holds a high position for poetically rendering the illimitable aspects of nature and the picturesqueness of rustic or Old World scenery and ruins. Under the guidance of his facile pencil how many have been instructed in art, and learned of the varied loveliness of this beautiful world! Thomas Moran ranks with Mr. Fenn as a master in this field. It appears to us that in this branch he displays more originality and imagination than in the elaborate paintings by which he is best known.

Within a very few years—so recently, in fact, that it is difficult to see where they came from—a school of *genre* illustrators have claimed recognition in our art, educated altogether in this country, and yet combining more art qualities in their works than we find in the same number of artists in any other department of American art. It is a little singular that, notwithstanding the recent interest in black and white in this country, the *genre* artists who represent it should at once have reached an excellence which commands admiration on both sides of the Atlantic, while our painters in the same department have rarely achieved more than a secondary rank.

Alfred Fredericks has distinguished himself by combining landscape and figure in a most graceful, airy style; and Miss Jessie Curtis, in the delineation of the simplicity and beauty of child life, has delightfully treated one of the most winsome subjects which can attract the pencil of the poetic artist. Miss Humphreys, in the choice of a somewhat similar class of subjects, has yet developed individuality of method marked by breadth of effect and forcible treatment. Of the ladies who have found scope for their abilities in the field of illustration perhaps none have excelled Mrs. Mary Halleck Foote. We cannot always find her style of composition agreeable, and in invention or lightness of fancy she seems deficient, while her manner is strong rather than graceful. But she is a most careful student of nature, and the effects she aims at, and sometimes reaches, are inspired by an almost masculine nerve and pow-

SOME ART CONNOISSEURS.—[W. HAMILTON GIBSON.]

er, and show knowledge and reserve force. Some of her realistic landscapes are almost as true and intense in black and white as the daring realisms of Courbet in color, but showing fine technical facility rather than imagination. Miss Annette Bishop, who died too early to win a general recognition of her talents, was gifted with a most delicate poetic fancy, and singular facility in giving expression to its dreams.

F. S. Church is an artist of imagination, painting in oil and water-colors, but perhaps best known for striking and weird compositions in black and white, often treating of animal or bird life. He is an artist whose advent into our art we hail with pleasure, not because his style is wholly matured or always quite satisfactory, for it is neither, but because it is inspired by a genuine art feeling, and yet more because it shows him to be —what so few of our artists have been—an idealist. What is art but a reaching out after the ideal, the most precious treasure given to man in this world? It includes faith, hope, and charity. To search after the ideal good, to live in an ideal world, to yearn after and try to create the harmony of the ideal, is the one boon left to man to give him a belief in immortality and a higher life. The more of an idealist the poet or the artist, the nearer he comes to fulfilling his mission. The idealist is the creator, the man of genius; and therefore we hail with joy the appearance of every idealist who enters our art ranks, and infuses vitality into the prose of technical art, and inspiration into the dogmas of the schools. The most hopeless feature of American art has always been hitherto, as with our literature, the too evident absence of imagination; and wherever we recognize an idealist, we set him down as another mile-stone to mark the progress in art. It is through the idealists that Heaven teaches truth to man; and hence another reason why we regard with such importance the present school of artists in black and white. In no department is there more scope for the imagination than in the drawing of the pure line or in the suggestions of *chiaro-oscuro*. Therein lies the enormous power of the art of Rembrandt. He dealt with that seemingly simple but really inexhaustible medium, light and shade: in the hands of a master, potent as the wand of a magician to evolve worlds out of chaos.

Barry, Bensell, Shepherd, Davis (who is also known as a decorative artist), T. A. Richards, Eytinge, Frost, Merrill, Ipsen, Shirlaw, Lathrop, Lewis, Perkins, and Davison are other artists who have justly acquired repute for success in the department of black and white, or book illustration. Kelley has a sketchy style that is very effective, and of which the correct rendering on wood would have been well-nigh impossible with the old processes; but there is danger of carrying it to the verge of sen-

"WASHINGTON OPENING THE BALL."—[C. S. REINHART.]

sationalism. The facilities afforded by photographing a design on wood has seemed to be the occasion for aiding the development of a class of artist-authors who both write and illustrate their own articles for the magazines. How remarkably well this can be done is proved by such clever artists as Howard Pyle and W. Gibson, who display at once fertility of imagination and technical facility as draughtsmen. C. S. Reinhart has become widely known as one of the most versatile illustrators we have produced. Excelling as a draughtsman, he brings to his aid an active fancy that enables him vividly to realize the scenes he undertakes to represent; and he seems equally at home in the portrayal of quaint old-time scenes, or the brilliant costumes and characters of the present day, combined with forcible delineations of scenery. The Puritan damsel or the belle of Newport may alike be congratulated when Mr. Reinhart ushers them before us with the grace of a master. The success of this school of artists, who have made their mark in the department of illustration, has doubtless been due in part to the increasing study of the figure in this country, and the greater facilities afforded for drawing from the life. Most of these artists are young men, whose abilities have been vastly assisted by their studies in life schools, which it would have been well-nigh impossible for them to find in the earlier periods of our art. Although perhaps better noticed under the head of Ethics rather than of Æsthetics, we may allude to the surprising growth and influence of caricature-drawing in this country, represented by such able artists as Nast, Bellew, Kepler, or Cusack, as associated with the development of our black and white art.

An artist who seems to combine the qualities we see more or less represented by other artists in black and white, who has already accomplished remarkable results, and gives promise of even greater successes, we find in E. A. Abbey. It must be taken into consideration that he is still very young; that he now for the first time visits the studios and galleries of Europe; that his advantages for a regular art education have been very moderate, and that he is practically self-educated. And then compare with these disadvantages the amount and the quality of the illustrations he has turned out, and we see represented in him genius of a high order, combining almost inexhaustible creativeness, clearness and vividness of conception, a versatile fancy, a poetic perception of beauty, a quaint, delicate humor, a wonderful grasp of whatever is weird and mysterious, and admirable *chiaro-oscuro*, drawing, and composition. When we note such a rare combination of qualities, we cease to be surprised at the cordial recognition awarded his genius by the best judges, both in London and Paris, even before he had left this country.

If I have spoken strongly in favor of our school of illustrators, it is because I think such commendation has been rightly earned, and to withhold it when merited would be as unjust as to give censure when undeserved. Criticism need not necessarily be the essence of vitriol and gall, as some critics seem to imagine it to be. A jury is as much bound to approve the innocent as to condemn the guilty.

MUSEUM OF FINE ARTS, BOSTON.

In another department of our arts we also feel called to award praise to a degree that has never before been possible in the history of American art. I refer to the department of architecture. It is difficult to say exactly when the new movement toward a fuller expression of beauty in our civic and domestic building began; but we are conscious that about ten years ago what was for a time a mere vague feeling after more agreeable examples of architecture shaped itself into a definite and almost systematic impulse. The Chicago fire, and more especially the great fire in Boston, accelerated the action of the forces that already directed the people to demand nobler forms and types in the constructions that were henceforth to be erected in our growing cities. The advance of landscape-gardening, as evidenced in the Central Park of New York, and the public parks of other cities, doubtless aided to increase the yearning for material beauty. But whatever the influences at work, there is no question as to the results already apparent. I would not be understood as approving all the buildings of importance that have recently been put up in this country—very far from it. But, on the other hand, one cannot avoid seeing that the general tendency is toward improved styles, and that here and there groups of buildings or single structures have been erected which are at once elegant, commodious, and artistic; and, if not strictly offering new orders of architecture, presenting at least graceful adaptations of old orders to new climatic and social conditions in a way that gives them the merit of originality.

So prominent has this improvement in architecture already become in American cities, that already their external aspect or profile has begun to partake of the picturesque character hitherto supposed to belong only to the Old World, and to present that massing of effect so dear to the artistic eye. We can illustrate this by mentioning only two or three examples among many. One who looks toward Philadelphia from the railway station on the east side of the Schuylkill, may see a cluster of spires and domes centering around the Academy of Fine Arts, which is so agreeably composed that one would almost imagine the position of each to be the deliberate choice of a master in composition. Twenty years ago one would have looked in vain for any such harmonious outline of structural beauty in this country. The small, quaint fishing-port of Marblehead has also found itself suddenly transformed into one of the most pleasing cities of the Union, as viewed from the Neck across the harbor; for on the very crest of the hills upon which the place is built a town-hall has been erected, of brick, neatly faced with stone, and surmounted by an elegant tower. At once the old town has emerged from the commonplace into the region of the picturesque. The new structure has given character and symmetrical outline to the city by producing convergence to a central point of effect; and when the sun sets behind it, and brings its outline into bold but harmonious relief against a golden background, while a mist of glowing rays glazes the whole into tone, the view is in the highest degree artistic, and so resembles some of the scenes one so often sees in the Old World that he can hardly believe he is gazing at an American prospect.

We find a somewhat similar effect, but on a much larger scale, presented by the new Capitol, or State-house, at Albany. This city, as beheld from the opposite banks of the Hudson at Greenbush, has always been one of the most pleasing of American cities, situated as it is on several lofty hills, divided by ravines in which purple shadows linger when night is approaching; but the addition of the vast structure now in course of completion there adds greatly to the glory of the spectacle. It dominates over the city of eighty thousand inhabitants with superb dignity; and the whole place borrows beauty from it, and is elevated above prose into poetry. Again one is reminded of the cathedral towns of Europe, where some lofty, venerable minster guards through the ages the roofs that cluster below. Not that this pile, which is rather hybrid in its style, is to be considered equal to the masterpieces of old-time architecture; but it is a long step in advance compared with the civic buildings formerly erected and admired in our cities, and its presence at the capital of a great State cannot but have an ennobling and educational influence upon rising generations.

The styles, whether pure or modified, that are most employed by our architects in this new movement have been chiefly the Romanesque, the Palladian Renaissance, the French Renaissance of Mansard and Perrault, and the later Elizabethan or Jacobean. The first two have entered chiefly into the construction of civic buildings; the second has been followed in religious edifices; while the last has been used with excellent effect in domestic architecture. A fine example of the success achieved in the employment of the Romanesque is seen in the new Trinity Church on the Back Bay lands, in Boston, designed by Gambrel and Richardson. This is one of the most conscientious and meritorious buildings erected on this continent, although less imposing than it would have been if the original design had been fully carried out. There is, also, an affectation of strength in the massive blocks of undressed stone under the windows, in a part where such strength is disproportionate to that employed in other portions of the building. But the general effect is excellent, and the covered approaches or cloisters are quite in the spirit of true architecture. Color enters judiciously into the selection of the stone used to aid the general effect; and the same observation may be applied to the very elegant tower of the new Old South Church, close at hand, designed by Peabody and Robinson, in the Italian Gothic style, and which for grace, beauty,

"THE ASTONISHED ABBÉ."—[E. A. ABBEY.]

and majesty has not been surpassed on this side of the Atlantic. The church edifice to which it is attached, although sufficiently ornate—perhaps too much so—is lacking in that repose of outline or just proportions that are required to bring it into harmony with the campanile.

Other towers and churches are clustered in that neighborhood, erected within ten years, which present an effect that is really intrinsically beautiful, without taking at all into question the rapidity of the transformation which has come over the spirit of our architecture. And the effect is heightened, to a degree never before attained on this continent since the Mound-builders passed away, by the excellence of the domestic architecture which has entered into the construction of the dwellings of that vicinage, especially on Boylston Street and the adjacent avenues. Beauty, taste, and comfort are there found combined to a degree that promises much for the future of architecture in our country. The gargoyles, gables, cornices, and carvings one meets at every turn carry one quite back to the Middle Ages. It is interesting to observe that the sham cornices formerly so common here are gradually being discarded, together with all the other trumpery decoration so much in vogue. Good honest work is shown in external decoration, together with a feeling for color that is adding much to the cheerfulness of our cities. Brick is made to do service for ornamentation as well as for mere dead walls, and string courses, or bands of colored tiles or terra-cotta carvings, all of an enduring character, enter into the external decorations of private dwellings.

Not only is the love of beauty shown in domestic architecture, but it is found displayed in the construction of banks and stores; and it is again in Boston that we find whole streets of buildings of rich and elegant design, and conscientiously constructed, devoted wholly to business purposes. But a building which, perhaps, more than any other is typical of the architectural movement now passing over the country is the Museum of Fine Arts in Boston. It is not so much after any one style as a choice from different schools of later Gothic adapted to modern conditions. The terra-cotta groups in relievo in the façade, temper what would be otherwise too large an expanse of warm color, for it is built of red brick. The grouped arches, turrets, and oriel windows, and the numerous terra-cotta decorations at the angles and on the gables, are elegant, but perhaps so generally distributed as to be a little confusing. The effect is scattered, and thus weakened, instead of being massed at one or two central or salient points. This is the most glaring error we discover in the present importation or adaptation of foreign and ancient styles to our needs here. It is an error which we share with the modern British architect, and was forcibly illustrated in the new Houses of Parliament, by Sir Charles Barry.

A CHILD'S PORTRAIT.—[B. C. PORTER.]

No buildings of this century are so profusely ornate as some of the magnificent cathedrals and town-halls of the Middle Ages; but at the same time all this sumptuousness of decoration was massed upon one or two effective spots, surrounded by large spaces comparatively simple and free of embellishment. Thus grandeur and nobility of outline were preserved, while extraordinary beauty in color and sculpture could be added without disturbing the general effect or cloying the imagination. But our architects, not having yet fully grasped the ideas after which they are searching, scatter instead of concentrating the external decorations of their buildings.

Interior decoration has also naturally assumed importance as the quality of our architecture has advanced. Elaborate wood-carvings are entering into the decorations of the houses of our citizens, and painting is called in to adorn the walls of private and civic buildings, sometimes with more affectation or extravagance than taste; although it can be conceded without hesitation that a remarkable and decided improvement is noticeable within a very few years in the decoration of interiors in this country. M. Brumidi made a beginning, some twenty years ago, in the frescoes of the Capitol at Washington; and quite recently Mr. Lafarge has beautified

A BIT OF VENICE.—[SAMUEL COLMAN.]

the interior of Trinity Church, Boston, and other public buildings, with sacred designs in fresco, and other decorative work in gold and red, which are very interesting. Among the last, and probably the most important, works of the late William M. Hunt were the mural paintings in oil for the new State-house at Albany. Other artists who have shown promise in this department are Francis Lathrop and Frank Hill Smith.

It is not surprising to find that this advance in decorative art, together with the increasing luxury accompanying it, should create a demand and develop a talent for toreutic art, or art in metal-work, especially the precious metals; and such we find to be the case. The success achieved in this department is, perhaps, the most remarkable yet attained in American art, excepting possibly that of some of our artists in black and white, and has justly merited and obtained unqualified applause abroad as well as at home. It is to such designers as Messrs. Grosjean, Perring, Wilkinson, and Moore, assisted by the most skilled artisans of the age, that our toreutic art is indebted for the recognition it received at the French Exposition.

Another sign of the rapidly increasing activity of the interest taken in the art question in America is presented by the art museums or galleries which have almost simultaneously arisen in Boston, New Haven, New York, and Washington, founded at considerable expense, and entirely without State aid. With the former two are connected important schools for art instruction, combined with fine casts of the masterpieces of ancient plastic art.

Another evidence of the awakening art feeling of a great nation is the demand for art education—a want which has been met by the establishment of numerous schools or academies of art in our leading cities all over the land, from the Atlantic to the Pacific. It is true that in Philadelphia, Boston, and New York academies were founded early in the century, and the last especially had become a very important factor in stimulating the latent love for art in our people. The Massachusetts Normal Art School, under the able direction of Mr. Walter Smith, while devoted chiefly to the advancement of industrial art, has also by its example greatly assisted the growth of the art feeling in the popular mind. While much may be urged with reason against compulsory instruction of art in the public schools, it would seem that few could be found to object to the education of art instructors, and the addition of an optional art branch to the State schools for the benefit of those who are desirous of art instruction, but are too poor to avail themselves of the advantages offered by such admirable art schools as those of the Cooper Institute and Artists' League in New York, the National Academy or the Museum of Fine Arts in Boston, or the Academy in Philadelphia. It may, then, be conceded that the founding of the Massachusetts Normal Art School is not only a strong indication of a growing demand, but that it has also been a very powerful agent in the diffusion of art knowledge in the United States.

Thus we see that by a cumulative effort the arts are making sudden and rapid progress in America. And there is still another movement which strikingly indicates this. Slow to be recognized, and meeting in some quarters with but cold welcome, it is yet by no means the least significant indication out of many that we are in the full tide of æsthetic progress, and have fairly entered on the third period of American art.

"THE OLD ORCHARD."—[R. SWAIN GIFFORD.]

From the time of West it has been not uncommon for our painters to go to Europe for study and observation; but they either had the misfortune to form their style after that of schools already conventional and on the wane, or they were not yet sufficiently advanced to accept the methods and principles of new masters and schools. A possible explanation, that is more philosophical, but which some may decline to accept, may be found in the general laws directing human progress, that obliged us, unconsciously, falteringly to tread one after the other the successive steps which others have followed before us. For the same reason, when an artist of unusual ability, like Stuart, appeared in the country, he had little or no following, because he came before his time.

A LANDSCAPE.—[GEORGE INNESS.]

But it has been evident for some years that a new element was entering our art ranks and demanding expression, which has at last reached a degree of vigor and organized strength that challenges respectful attention, if not unqualified acceptance. By associations, schools, and exhibitions of its own, it has thrown down the gauntlet to conservatism and conventionalism, and the time has arrived when we can no longer shut our eyes to the fact that a new force is exerting itself with iconoclastic zeal to introduce a different order of things into American art. We cannot justly consider this movement in the light of reform, for up to this time our art has been very creditable, and, considering the environing circumstances, full as advanced proportionally as the other factors of American civilization. We regard it simply as another stage in our art progress, destined, when it has accomplished its end, to be in turn succeeded by yet higher steps in the scale of advance; for, notwithstanding the somewhat demonstrative assumptions of some of its promoters, the new movement does not comprehend within itself, more than any other school, all the qualities of great art. To no school of art has it yet been given to demonstrate and include in itself all the possibilities of art, or to interpret all the truths of nature and man. Perhaps some future school may arise, with all the knowledge of the ages to choose from, which may comprehend the whole sphere of art in its compass. But they are probably not yet born who shall see it, or give to it the symmetry of perfection. Until that time, it behooves those neophytes and disciples, who proclaim that their art includes all that art has to tell, to be modest in their claims, and to be satisfied if they have been able by fasting and prayer to enrich the

"LA MARGUERETTE—THE DAISY."—[WILLIAM M. HUNT.]

world of art with one or two new truths. Nowhere is humility more becoming than in art; arrogance and assumption dig its grave sooner or later; while humility is by no means incompatible with earnestness, zeal, and progress.

The ripeness of our art for a change before the new movement actually assumed definite shape had already been suggested and welcomed in advance by such artists as Eastman Johnson, Homer Martin, and Samuel

Colman, the admirable painter in oil and water colors, strong in *chiaroscuro*, brilliant in color, and, although without academic training abroad, of a most excellent catholic spirit in all matters relating to art, ready to accept the good of whatever school, and to aid progress in the arts of his native land by whomsoever promoted. Benjamin C. Porter, whose massive characterizations in portraiture, broadly treated and admirably colored, have been among the most important achievements in recent American art, and Winslow Homer, A. H. Wyant, and E. M. Bannister are also among the artists whose sympathies are naturally with the new movement, although receiving their art training chiefly in this country, and who have thus indicated and prepared the way for the assertion of new influences in our art.

R. Swain Gifford should be added to the list of the noteworthy landscape-painters who have thrown the weight of their influence in advance to welcome to our shores new elements of progress and change whereby to quicken American art to fresh conquests. This artist at one time devoted his efforts to marine-painting, in which he did and still does some creditable work, his knowledge of ships being sufficiently technical to satisfy the nautical eye; but since his sojourn in Algeria, and the observations made in the Continental galleries and studios, he has devoted himself to landscape, and adopted a bolder style and a truer scheme of color. The influence of French art is perceptible in his later methods, but altogether as an influence, and in no sense as an imitation, for in his works there is always evident a sturdy self-assertion, whether in subject or treatment. In catching the gray effects of brooding skies receding in diminishing ranks through an aërial perspective of great distance and space, and giving with fine feeling the Druid-like spirit of clumps of sombre russet-hued cedars moaning by the granite shore of old Massachusetts, and identifying himself with the mysterious thoughts they suggest, Mr. Gifford has no superior on this side of the Atlantic. As a professor in the Cooper Institute, his influence is of great importance to the future of American pictorial art.

George Inness is another painter who, although without training in foreign studios, should be included with the artists just named, whose sympathies have gradually led him to exemplify in his works some of the most characteristic traits of later Continental methods. At first his style was not unlike the prevailing style of our middle school of landscape-painting; like that, giving careful attention to the reproduction of details. But his emotional nature, and intense reflection upon the philosophical principles of art, gradually led him to a broader style and a more free expression of the truths of nature, dealing with masses rather than with details, and handling his subjects — especially atmospheric effects — with a daring and an insight that has never been surpassed in our landscape art. To these he has added a feeling for light and color that place him, at his best, among the masters of the art. But there is inequality in his works,

MOONLIGHT.—[JOHN J. ENNEKING.]

and sometimes a conflict of styles, as when he dashes off a composition, in two or three sittings, that is full of fire and suggestion; and then, perhaps with a relic of his first method still lingering in his memory like a habit, goes over it again, and smooths away some of those bold touches which, to an imaginative observer, gave it additional force.

In his latest works Mr. Inness has shown a disposition to yield more and more to a style at present called impressionist. Impressionism pure and simple, as represented by its most extravagant supporters, is like trying to represent the soul without the body. This may be well enough in another world; but in this a material body is needed to give it support. But,

"HAVING A GOOD TIME."—[LOUIS C. TIFFANY.]

philosophically considered, there is no question that impressionism—or the attempt to represent nature according to the impressions it makes upon the mind's eye, rather than the mere reflections left on the material eye—undoubtedly presents the quintessence of the spirit of art; and therefore all good art must have in it more or less evidence of subjective influence. But just so long as art finds expression with material means, the artist must make concessions to the limitations of substance. Naturally, of all the arts, music comes nearest to the ideal which the impressionist is seeking to grasp.

It is useless to deny that, extravagant as some of the works of the contemporary impressionists appear to many, they undoubtedly present a keen appreciation of aërial chromatic effects, and for this reason are worthy of careful attention. That they are not carried nearer to completion, however, indicates a consciousness on the part of the artist that he is as yet unable to harmonize the objective and subjective, the material and the spiritual phases of art. A perfect work of art combines the two; but, alas! such achievements are as yet rare, although that is the ideal which the artist should keep in view. The artist who gives us what is called a finished painting is so far right. He represents what appears to the material eye. In proportion as he combines with this a suggestion of the intellectual impression also made on his mental vision, he approaches the ideal in art execution. On the other hand, the artist who is impatient of details, and deals wholly with a broad, and sometimes, we regret to say, daubv and slovenly interpretation of nature, is yet so far right, because he is endeavoring to interpret the wholly imaginative and intellectual side of art. When to this bias he adds the balance of power which enables him to give something of the other phase of art, he in turn approaches the ideal aim of art. Turner was an impressionist; so was Corot; so, to go farther back, was Velasquez; so, also, are the Japanese. But these artists, especially Turner and Velasquez, had the supreme faculty of uniting the two opposite poles in art in their best works, and hence the commanding position which they hold, and always will hold, in the art world.

SOUTHAMPTON, LONG ISLAND.—[C. H. MILLER.]

So far as can be ascertained, it is to the late William M. Hunt that we must ascribe the initiation of the third period in our pictorial art, and perhaps, in a secondary manner, the general impulse toward foreign styles now modifying the arts of design in this country. When Mr. Hunt went to Düsseldorf to study, in 1846, he did no more than many of our artists had already done. But when, dissatisfied with the conventionalism of that school, he turned his steps to Paris, and became a pupil of Couture, and was one of the first to discover, to admire, and to emulate the art methods of Millet, then, unconsciously, he became a power, destined by his somewhat narrow but intense personality to influence the destinies of our art—especially by returning to Boston, a city easily brought under the magnetism of a strong individuality, and more ready than any other city in the land to surrender the guidance of its opinions to those whom it condescends to admire.

The going of Mr. Hunt to Paris meant that technical knowledge and the perception of the underlying principles of art were now, as never before, to be systematically mastered and imported to America by our artists, together with the most advanced theories, truths, or discoveries in the technical part of the subject. It did not mean that all our artists who went abroad to study would necessarily be great, or that any of them would be especially original, but that there would be a general harmony of action toward improving the means of art education in America. Regarded in this light, Mr. Hunt must be considered to have been a most important promoter of the development of art in America. He was probably not a man of genius—unless great force of character be considered as such—but he had a true perception of the character and aims, the limitations and possibilities of art; and the intolerance he sometimes exhibited was not unusual in those who are introducing new methods, and have to create a circle of influence. In his own works, as a landscape, portrait, *genre*, and decorative painter, it cannot be said that he added greatly to the sum of the world's art by anything strikingly original; but he exhibited a true perception of the importance of the ideal in art; and one feels, in contemplating his works, that he was ever striving to overcome the difficulties of material means of expressing the ideal. Moved, like most leading American painters, by a feeling for color rather than for form, yet, in such compositions as "The Bathers," representing a boy about to dive from the shoulders of another, who is half immersed in a pool, vanishing into the green gloom of the wooded banks, we have an admirable example of the manner in which this artist sometimes combined form, *chiaro-oscuro*, and color, with a delicacy, force, and suggestion of outline and tint, to a degree rarely equalled before by American art; with a technique essentially that of the later French school, yet modified by individual feeling.

But the life-work of Mr. Hunt was, after all, not more in his paintings than in that influence by which he gathered about him a school of admirers and disciples who disseminated his opinions and imitated his style, although rarely with his success. Among those who directly profited by his style and influence may be mentioned Mrs. Darrah, who effectively paints gray coast scenes and landscapes in a low, minor key; Miss Helen

A STUDY.—[FREDERICK DIELMAN.]

M. Knowlton; Miss Bartol; F. P. Vinton; and S. S. Tuckerman, the marine painter.

The power of Mr. Hunt was still more widely felt in directing a large number of young art-students to visit Paris, and eventually also Munich, at each of which the tendency has been for some years toward bolder methods in the technics of art. The result has been to introduce to this country a truer perception of the vital importance of style in the present stage of our art, and to emphasize the truth that he who has anything to say will make it much more effective if he knows how to give it adequate utterance.

Of the many Boston artists who have profited by foreign study and are now resident in that city, we can mention but three or four. John J. Enneking, a graduate of the studios of Munich and Paris, can hardly be called an idealist. There is little evidence of imagination in his canvases; but in seizing the effects of the brilliant lights of sunset, or the varied grays of a lowering sky on a cloudy day, he shows himself equally happy in color, *chiaro-oscuro*, and technical skill in handling pigments. His versatility is remarkable. He can render the figure from life with a vigor and freshness scarcely less than that of his landscapes. There is, unfortunately, an evidence of haste in too many of his works, which cannot be too much regretted, for he thus fails to do justice to the very decided ability he possesses. Having studied both in Munich and Paris, and given careful attention to all the European schools of art, and adding to this knowledge sturdy independence of opinion and great earnestness and energy, Mr. Enneking ought to be strongly influential in the present stage of American art.

We find much that is interesting in the paintings of E. L. Weeks. They are marked by a powerful individuality, which delights in glowing effects of light, and revels in the brilliant coloring of tropical scenery or the varied splendor of Oriental architecture and costumes. There is something Byronic in the fervor of this artist's enthusiasm for the East, and the easy adaptability that has enabled a son of New England to identify himself with the life and scenery of lands so exactly the opposite of his own. Although a pupil of Bonnat, and an ardent admirer of the excessive realism now affected by some of the followers of the later French school, Mr. Weeks is, in spite of himself, an idealist, and no imitator of any style. This has, perhaps, been an injury to him, for he finds difficulty in mastering the technical or mechanical problems of his profession. A lack of knowledge or feeling for form, a weakness in drawing which is too often perceptible in his works, and sometimes an apparent opaqueness in his pigments, impair the quality of compositions which are inspired by the fire of genius.

J. M. Stone, who is one of the professors at the Museum of Fine Arts, and a graduate of the Munich schools, indicates considerable force in rendering the figure, both in color and drawing, and a touch of genius in the

"THE BURGOMASTER."—[H. MUHRMAN.]

painting of dogs and horses. His service in the army during the war intensified his interest in equine art, and will probably result in important compositions suggested by that conflict. C. R. Grant has a delicate poetic feeling for color and form, and a pleasant fancy tinged with quaintness; and in his choice of treatment and subject suggests the works of G. H. Boughton. In T. W. Dewing, a pupil of Lefévre, who has recently settled in Boston, we find much promise in figure-painting, but altogether after the clear-cut, well-drawn, but somewhat dry method of Gérôme.

J. Foxcroft Cole, who has been a careful student of the best phases of French landscape art, but has formed, at the same time, a sufficiently individual style of his own, is an artist whose works command a growing esteem. Although adding groups of cattle to his compositions, he is essentially a landscape-painter. We receive from a study of his works an impression of sameness, like that conveyed by the landscapes of Corot, chiefly because they are generally on one key, and refer to a class of subjects so quiet and undemonstrative that only he who observes them repeatedly and reflectively discovers that each work is the result of a distinct inspiration, and possesses suggestions and qualities of its own. Exquisite feeling for space and atmosphere, for the peaceful effects of pastoral life, and the more subtle aspects of nature, especially in color, are the characteristics of the style of Mr. Cole.

In reviewing the Boston school, we note in its development much activity and earnestness, too often combined, however, with crudeness; while the foreign influence that is, on the whole, most evident in it is that of the contemporary French school. As Boston is intense rather than broad in its intellectual traits, and is inclined to follow the lead of its own first thinkers and artists, it is the more unfortunate that one influence should predominate, because in such a case the errors as well as the good qualities of a style are liable to receive too much attention; while free growth depends on the catholic eclecticism which supplements the study of nature by culling the good from different schools, and correcting one by comparison with another, thus enabling the artist to arrive at a more just and profound view of a question that proceeds upon irreversible laws. The mind thus educated learns by balancing the merits of different schools, and the results are not so much imitation as assimilation, yielding healthy growth and development.

In New York there seems to be, with no less activity than that of

Boston, an art movement which is based on broader grounds, and offers more encouragement for the future of our art. The artists who are the most influential in this advance are more equally divided between the French and the German schools than those of Boston, and indicate more breadth of sympathy and art culture, together with a cosmopolitan love for the good in the art of all schools, which is one of the most encouraging

"BURIAL OF THE DEAD BIRD."—[J. ALDEN WIER.]

of signs in a dawning intellectual reform. So decided had the tendency toward Munich become soon after 1870, that the colony of American art students in Munich soon grew sufficiently large to establish an art association, having stated days of meeting, at which contributed paintings were exhibited and discussed, and carefully prepared papers on art topics were read. Opinions were exchanged in this manly, earnest, sympathetic man-

"THE APPRENTICE."—[WILLIAM M. CHASE.]

ner, and breadth and catholicity were reached in the consideration of the great question in which all were so profoundly interested. Thus were gained many of the influences which are destined to affect American art for ages to come.

The writer regards as among the most improving and delightful evenings he has enjoyed those passed with some of these talented and enthusiastic art students at the table where a number regularly met to dine—at the Max Emanuel café in Munich. Dinner over, huge flagons of beer were placed before each one, and pipes were lit, whose wreaths of upward-curling smoke softened the gleam of the candles, and gave a poetic haze to the dim nooks of the hall that was highly congenial to the hour and the topics discussed. The leonine head of Duveneck, massively set on his broad shoulders, as from time to time behind a cloud of smoke he gave forth an opinion, lent much dignity to the scene; while the grave, thoughtful features of Shirlaw, and the dreamy, contemplative face of Chase, occasionally lit by a flash of impetuous emotion, aided by an eloquent gesture, made the occasion one of great interest. Others there were around the board whose sallies of humor or weighty expressions of opinion made an indelible impression.

Among the resident artists of New York who have recently studied abroad, Louis C. Tiffany, a follower of the French school, holds a prominent position. He has done some very clever things in landscape and *genre* from subjects suggested by his trip to the East, and has succeeded equally in oil and water colors, and is now giving a preference to American subjects, and also turning his attention to the pursuit of decorative art. He is essentially a colorist, to whom the radiant tints of the iris seem like harmoniously chorded strains of music. William Sartain, a pupil of Bonnât and Yvon, has also proved himself an excellent colorist, and shows vigor and truth of drawing both in figure and architectural perspective, as well as pleasing composition in work which he has done abroad.

The new phase into which our landscape art is passing under foreign influence is well indicated by the paintings of Charles Miller, a graduate of the Munich school, who is inspired by a stirring, breezy love for nature, especially for her more intense and vivid effects, strong contrasts of light and shade, glowing sunsets, and masses of dun gray clouds rolling up in thunderous majesty and gloom over landscapes fading off into the infinite distance. As a draughtsman Mr. Miller is less interesting than in rendering such effects as we have suggested with broad, free handling, in which he is often very successful. He is a poet moved by a powerful imagination, idealizing what he sees, and possessed of a memory similar to that of Turner; and thus some of his most striking canvases are the result of a tenacious memory allied to a vigorous observation. Some of his canvases suggest the landscapes of Constable.

"THE PROFESSOR."—[THOMAS EAKINS.]

Frederick Dielman, who has pursued his studies in Munich, is destined to make his mark in *genre*. In color and tone, and especially in drawing, he has already shown decided ability, and some of his compositions are very promising. Messrs. Weir and Muhrman, both young artists of much promise, and both figure-painters, represent the influence of two different schools. The former comes from an artistic family, his father being Robert W. Weir, one of our oldest painters. Young J. Alden Weir studied in Paris. In portraiture he has a remarkable faculty for seizing

"THE GOOSE-HERD."—[WALTER SHIRLAW.]

character, painting the eye with a truth and life wholly original. In *genre* he is sometimes quite successful, although inclined to mannerism. Mr. Muhrman is from Cincinnati, and has spent two years in Munich. While there, he placed himself under no master, but observed keenly, and devoted himself wholly to water-colors. Avoiding the use of body color, he yet shows dash and originality in technique, and a fine eye for form and color. The realistic vigor of his work is quite exceptional among our water-color painters. The brilliance and purity of his colors, and the delicious *abandon* with which he handles the brush to such admirable result, seem to promise that he will become a master in this art. Frank Waller, Wyatt Eaton, W. A. Low, A. P. Ryder, J. H. Twachtman, J. C. Beckwith, A. F. Bunner, Miss Helena De Kay, and Miss M. R. Oakey are among the leading artists who are aiding the new art movement in New York.

But among the later influences which have entered into our art and promise striking results, there is none more worthy of our consideration than the return of Messrs. Shirlaw and Chase from a thorough course of study in Germany. One of the points of most importance in this connection is that whereas our art for the last thirty years has been in the direction of landscape, its tendencies are now rather toward the painting of the figure, and this is strikingly illustrated by the circumstance that both of these artists have done their strongest work in this department, and their influence will undoubtedly give a fresh impulse to figure-painting. Mr. Shirlaw was for a year professor in the Students' League, but has now abandoned teaching in order that nothing may interfere with original work. Trained in the school which has produced such artists as Defregger, Diez, Braith, and Brandt, he has mastered all the technical knowledge which Munich can give an artist in *genre* in our day. There is no uncertainty or weakness in his method of handling color; his lines are clearly and carefully drawn, and he undoubtedly achieves excellent results when he attempts simple compositions. One of Mr. Shirlaw's best known compositions, representing a sheep-shearing in Bavaria, has attracted favorable attention at home and abroad. In compositions which include animals, dogs, and birds, he has been especially happy. His inclinations to delineate the characteristics of bird-life are akin to those of the artists of Japan.

The genius of Mr. Chase is rather for single figures than elaborate compositions; and his independence of action is shown by the fact that, although he studied with Piloty, the master whom he made his model of excellence was Velasquez. A noble sense of color is perceptible in all his works, whether in the subtle elusive tints of flesh, or in the powerful

"A SPANISH LADY."—[MISS MARY S. CASSATT.]

rendering of a mass of scarlet, as in his notable painting of the "Court Jester." In the painting of a portrait he endeavors, sometimes very successfully, to seize character, although occasionally rather too impressionist in style. His art-life is fired by a lively enthusiasm, which must result in genuine and exalted art. "Waiting for the Ride" is a fine, thoughtful ideal figure of a lady by this artist.

In Philadelphia the new movement has some powerful allies, among whom should be prominently mentioned Thomas Eakins, a pupil of Gérôme, and at present professor in the Philadelphia Academy of Art. One of Mr. Eakins's most ambitious paintings represents a surgical operation before a class in anatomy. It is characterized by so many excellent artistic qualities, that one regrets that the work as a whole fails to satisfy. Admirable draughtsman as this painter is, one is surprised that in the arrangement of the figures the perspective should have been so ineffective that the mother is altogether too small for the rest of the group, and the figure of the patient so indistinct that it is difficult to tell exactly the part of the body upon which the surgeon is performing the operation. The monochromatic tone of the composition is, perhaps, intentional, in order to concentrate the effect on the bloody thigh and the crimson finger of the operating professor. But as it is, the attention is at once and so entirely directed on that reeking hand as to convey the impression that such con-

STUDY OF A BOY'S HEAD.—[W. SARTAIN.]

centration was the sole purpose of the painting. In similar paintings by Ribeira, Regnault, and other artists of the horrible, as vivid a result is obtained without sacrificing the light and color in the other parts of the picture; and the effect, while no less intense, is, therefore, less staring and loud. As to the propriety of introducing into our art a class of subjects hitherto confined to a few of the more brutal artists and races of the Old World, the question may well be left to the decision of the public. In color Mr. Eakins effects a low tone that is sometimes almost monochromatic, but has very few equals in the country in drawing of the figure. Some of his portraits are strongly characteristic, and give remarkable promise. Miss Emily Sartain is devoting herself with good success to *genre* and portraiture; and Miss Mary Cassatt merits more extended notice and earnest praise for the glory of color and the superb treatment and composition of some of her works.

When we review the various forces now actively at work to hasten forward the progress of American art, we see that they are, with one or two exceptions, still immature; while, on the other hand, the sum of their influence is such as to prove that they are already sufficiently well established to give abundant promise of vitality, and of a career of success that seems destined to carry the arts to a degree of excellence never before seen in America. While the ideal is a more prominent feature of our art than formerly, the tide also sets strongly toward realism, together with a clearer practical knowledge of technique. And while we do not discover marked original power in the artists who represent the new movement, we find in them a self-reliance and a sturdiness of purpose which renders them potential in establishing the end they have in view. It is to their successors that we must look for the founding of a school that shall be at once native in origin, and powerful in the employment of the material to express the ideal.

INDEX.

Abbey, E. A., 177.
Academy of Fine Arts (of New York), 24.
Akers, Benjamin Paul, 151.
Alexander, Cosmo, 16, 24.
Alexander, Francis, 49.
Allston, Washington, 16, 29, 31, 44, 47.
American Art Students' Association, Munich, 200.
Ames, Joseph, 49.
Andrew, John, 168.
Annin, P., 168.
Anthony, A. V. S., 168.
Architecture, 178.
Art Education, 186.
Artists' Funding Society, 88.
Artists' League, 186.
Athenæum, Providence, 31.
Augur, Hezekiah, 138.

Bacon, Henry, 7.
Baker, George A., 49.
Ball, Thomas, 149, 150.
Bannister, E. M., 106, 190.
Barry, Charles A., 174.
Bartholomew, Edward S., 152.
Bartol, E. H., 195.
Beard, James, 86.
Beard, William H., 86.
Beckwith, J. C., 207.
Bellew, Frank H. T., 177.
Bellows, A. F., 79.
Bensell, E. B., 174.
Benson, Eugene, 7.
Berkeley, Bishop, 15, 17.
Bierstadt, Albert, 97.
Birch, Thomas, 37.
Bishop, Annette, 174.
Bispham, Henry C., 86.

Blackburn, 16.
Blashfield, Edwin H., 7.
Blauvelt, C. F., 115.
Boutelle, D. W. C., 106.
Bowdoin College, paintings of, 47.
Brackett, Walter M., 85.
Bradford, William, 84.
Bricher, A. T., 111.
Bridgman, Frederick A., 7.
Bridges, Fidelia, 131.
Bristol, John B., 76.
Brown, George L., 64.
Brown, Harry, 84.
Brown, J. Appleton, 106.
Brown, J. G., 115.
Brown, J. H., 167.
Brown, J. Ogden, 131.
Browne, Henry K., 149.
Brumidi, M., 185.
Bunner, A. F., 207.
Burling, Gilbert, 112.
Burns, J., 115.

Calverly, Charles, 156.
Casilear, John W., 73.
Cassatt, Mary, 210.
Catlin, George, 88.
Champney, J. W., 113.
Chapman, J. G., 88.
Chase, William M., 203, 207.
Church, Frederick E., 81.
Church, F. S., 174.
Cincinnati, Music Hall of, 163.
Clevenger, Shobal Vail, 138, 145.
Close, A. P., 104.
Cobb, Darius, 125.
Cole, J., 168.
Cole, J. Foxcroft, 199.

212 INDEX.

Cole, Thomas, 47, 66.
Conant, Cornelia W., 7.
Colman, Samuel, 79, 112, 190.
Copley, John Singleton, 16, 17, 88, 138, 164.
Cooper Institute, 186.
Cranch, Christopher P., 76.
Crawford, Thomas, 138, 145, 149.
Cropsey, Jasper F., 76.
Cummings, T. S., 167.
Curtis, Jessie, 172.
Cusack, S., 177.
Custer, E. L., 125.

Dana, W. P. W., 7.
Dana, William J., 168.
Darley, Felix O. C., 171.
Darrah, Mrs. S. T., 195.
Davis, J. P., 168.
Davis, T. R., 174.
Davidson, Julian O., 174.
Deas, Charles, 88.
Decorative Art, 186.
De Haas, M. F. H., 109.
De Kay, Helena, 207.
Dengler, Frank, 161.
Dewing, T. W., 199.
Dexter, Henry, 156.
Dielman, Frederick, 204.
Dillon, Julia, 133.
Dix, Charles Temple, 84.
Dolph, J. H., 131.
Doughty, Thomas, 47, 56, 59, 66.
Drowne, Shem, 14, 37, 136.
Dunlap, William, 18.
Durand, Asher B., 47, 56, 59, 66, 167.
Duveneck, F., 7, 203.

Eakins, Thomas, 208.
Eaton, Wyatt, 207.
Edmonds, F. W., 52.
Elninger, John W., 115.
Elliott, Charles Loring, 49, 50.
Enneking, John J., 196.
Eytinge, Sol, 174.
Ezekiel, Moses J., 156.

Falconer, John M., 112.
Farrar, Henry, 113.
Fassett, Mrs. C. A., 127.
Feke, Robert, 16.
Fenn, Harry, 172.
Flagg, George B., 87.

Foote, Mrs. Mary Halleck, 172.
Fraser, John, 31, 56, 167.
Frazee, John, 136, 138.
Fredericks, Alfred, 172.
Freeman, Mrs. J. E., 156.
French, Daniel C., 161.
Frost, Arthur B., 174.
Frothingham, James, 27.
Fuller, George, 117.
Fuller, R. H., 76.
Furness, William Henry, 125.

Gardner, Elizabeth J., 7.
Gaul, Gilbert, 113.
Gerry, Samuel L., 74.
Gibson, W., 177.
Gifford, R. Swain, 112, 190.
Gifford, Sanford R., 80.
Goodrich, Sarah, 51, 167.
Gould, Thomas R., 152, 154.
Grant, C. R., 199.
Greenough, Horatio, 138, 142.
Greenough, Richard, 156.
Grey, Henry Peters, 51.
Grey, Mrs. Henry Peters, 125.
Grosjean, Charles T., 186.
Guy, S. J., 115.

Hale, Susan, 113.
Hall, Mrs., 167.
Hall, George H., 133.
Hamilton, James, 71, 84.
Harding, Chester, 47, 49.
Hart, James, 79, 130.
Hart, William, 79.
Hart, Joel T., 138, 145.
Hartley, J. S., 161.
Haseltine, H. J., 156.
Hayes, William, 85.
Heade, M. J., 133.
Healy, G. P. A., 49.
Henry, E. L., 115.
Henshaw, Mrs., 133.
Hicks, Thomas, 49, 86.
Hill, Thomas, 97, 98.
Hinckley, T. H., 85.
Homer, Winslow, 117, 190.
Hoppin, Augustus, 172.
Hoskin, Robert, 168.
Hosmer, Harriet, 152, 156.
Howland, A. C., 115.
Hubbard, R. W., 74.

Humphrey, L. B., 172.
Hunt, William M., 49, 185, 193.
Huntington, Daniel, 49, 51, 88.

IMPRESSIONISM in Art, 192.
Ingham, C. C., 49.
Inman, Henry, 49, 51.
Inness, George, 79, 190.
Inness, George, Jun., 131.
Ipsen, L. S., 174.
Irving, J. B., 113.
Ives, C. B., 156.

JARVIS, John Wesley, 28, 49.
Johnson, David, 76.
Johnson, Eastman, 116, 189.
Juengling, F., 168.

KELLEY, J. E., 174.
Kensett, John F., 63, 76.
Kepler, Joseph, 177.
Key, John R., 170.
King, F. S., 168.
Kingsley, E., 168.
Knowlton, Helen M., 193.
Kreul, G., 168.

LAFARGE, John, 71, 94, 133, 185.
Lambdin, George C., 133.
Lansil, Walter F., 111.
Lathrop, Francis, 96, 174, 186.
Lay, Oliver I., 115.
Le Clear, Thomas, 49.
Leutze, Emmanuel, 73, 88.
Lewis, Robert, 174.
Linton, W. J., 167.
Longfellow, Ernest, 106.
Longworth, Nicholas, 140.
Loop, Henry A., 125.
Loop, Mrs. Henry A., 125.
Low, Will H., 207.

MACDONALD, J. W. A., 156.
M'Entee, Jervis, 103.
Magrath, William, 117.
Malbone, Edward G., 31, 32, 167.
Marsh, Charles, 168.
Marshall, John, 167.
Martin, Homer, 106.
Mather, Cotton, 14.
Maverick, Peter, 167.
Mayer, B. F., 113.

Meade, Larkin J., 152, 153.
Meeker, J. R., 74.
Mignot, Louis R., 83.
Miller, Charles, 203.
Millet, Francis D., 7.
Mills, Clark, 138, 149.
Milmore, Martin, 154.
Moore, E. C., 186.
Moran, Edward, 103.
Moran, Peter, 103, 130.
Moran, Thomas, 97, 100, 172.
Morse, Samuel F. B., 33, 39, 51.
Morse, W. H., 168.
Mount, William Sidney, 52, 86, 117.
Muhrman, William H., 207.
Müller, R. A., 168.
Munzig, B. C., 170.
Museum of Fine Arts, Boston, 186.

NAEGLE, John, 29.
Nast, Thomas, 177.
National Academy of Design, 37, 39, 49, 51, 58, 186.
Neal, David, 7.
Newton, Gilbert Stuart, 27.
Nicoll, J. C., 111.
Normal Art School of Massachusetts, 186, 187.
Norton, William E., 110.

OAKEY, Maria R., 207.
O'Donovan, W. R., 161.

PAGE, William, 49, 51, 90.
Palmer, Erastus D., 140, 156, 161.
Parsons, Charles, 112.
Parton, Arthur, 80.
Parton, Ernest, 7.
Peale, Charles Wilson, 21.
Peale, Rembrandt, 28.
Pelham, 20.
Pennsylvania Academy of the Fine Arts, 29, 187.
Perkins, Charles, 174.
Perring, 186.
Petersen, John E. C., 110.
Pope, Alexander, 132.
Porter, Benjamin C., 190.
Powers, Hiram, 138.
Pratt, Matthew, 16, 137.
Pyle, Howard, 177.

QUARTLEY, Arthur, 111.

INDEX

Ranney, William S., 88.
Redwood Library, Newport, 15.
Reinhart, B. F., 115.
Reinhart, C. S., 177.
Reynolds, Joshua, 19.
Richards, T. Addison, 174.
Richards, William T., 74.
Rimmer, William, 163.
Rinehart, William Henry, 152, 154.
Ritchie, A. H., 167.
Robbins, Ellen, 133.
Robbins, Horace, 80.
Roberts, Howard, 161.
Robinson, Thomas, 130.
Rogers, Frank, 131.
Rogers, John, 159.
Rogers, Randolph, 149, 152.
Rothermel, Peter F., 88.
Rowse, Samuel W., 170.
Rush, William, 138.
Ryder, A. P., 207.

St. Gaudens, Augustus, 163.
Sargent, Colonel Henry, 28.
Sartain, Emily, 210.
Sartain, John, 167.
Sartain, William, 203.
Satterlee, Walter, 115.
Seavey, G. W., 133.
Shapleigh, F. H., 76.
Shirlaw, Walter, 174, 203, 207.
Shurtleff, R. M., 131.
Silva, Francis A., 111.
Simmons, Franklin, 154.
Smilie, George, 80.
Smilie, James, 167.
Smilie, James, Jun., 80, 113.
Smith, Frank Hill, 186.
Smith, J. Hopkinson, 171.
Smith, Walter, 186.
Smithwick and French, 168.
Smybert, John, 15, 22.
Sonntag, W. L., 79.
Staigg, Richard M., 49, 51.
Stebbins, Emma, 156.
Stephens, Louis, 172.
Stephenson, Peter, 156.
Stone, J. M., 196.
Story, George H., 118.
Story, William W., 152, 154.

Stuart, Gilbert, 17, 20, 24, 39, 47, 49, 187.
Sully, Thomas, 28, 49.
Suydam, James A., 73.

Tait, A. F., 132.
Thompson, Launt, 152, 159.
Thompson, Wordsworth, 128.
Thorpe, T. B., 86.
Tiffany, Louis C., 203.
Trumbull, Colonel John, 17, 21, 47, 88, 130, 136.
Tuckerman, S. S., 195.
Twachtman, J. H., 207.

Vanderlyn, John, 17, 29, 44.
Vandyck, Sir Anthony, 14.
Van Wart, Ames, 156.
Vedder, Elihu, 71, 94.
Volk, Leo W., 156.

Waldo, Samuel, 49.
Waller, Frank, 207.
Ward, J. Q. A., 149, 151.
Warner, Olin M., 161.
Water-Color Society, 112.
Waterman, Marcus, 113.
Watson, John, 15.
Way, A. J. H., 133.
Weeks, E. L., 196.
Weir, J. Alden, 204.
Weir, John F., 114.
Weir, Robert W., 47, 52.
West, Benjamin, 17, 29, 138, 142, 164.
Whistler, J. A. McN., 7.
Whitney, Anne, 156.
Whittredge, Worthington, 73, 86.
Wight, Moses, 7.
Wilkinson, George, 186.
Willard, A. W., 114.
Williams, F. D., 76.
Williams, Virgil, 115.
Wilmarth, Lemuel E., 115.
Wolf, H., 168.
Wood, T. W., 114.
Woodville, Richard Caton, 86.
Wright, Frederick W., 170.
Wright, Patience, 37, 136.
Wyant, A. H., 105, 190.

Young, Harvey A., 125.

THE END.

TIMELY AND IMPORTANT BOOKS
ON
ANCIENT AND MODERN ART.

American Art.
By S. G. W. Benjamin. Illustrated. 8vo, Cloth, $4 00.

Contemporary Art in Europe.
By S. G. W. Benjamin. Copiously Illustrated. Square 8vo, Cloth, Illuminated and Gilt, $3 50; Half Calf, $5 75.

Art Education Applied to Industry.
By George Ward Nichols. Illustrated. Square 8vo, Cloth, Illuminated and Gilt, $4 00.

Art Decoration Applied to Furniture.
By Harriet Prescott Spofford. Illustrated. Square 8vo, Cloth, Illuminated and Gilt, $4 00; Half Calf, $6 25.

Cyprus: its Ancient Cities, Tombs, and Temples.
A Narrative of Researches and Excavations during Ten Years' Residence in that Island. By General Louis Palma di Cesnola. With Portrait, Maps, and 400 Illustrations. 8vo, Cloth, Extra, Gilt Tops and Uncut Edges, $7 50.

Pottery and Porcelain
Of All Times and Nations. With Tables of Factory and Artists' Marks, for the Use of Collectors. By William C. Prime, LL.D. Illustrated. 8vo, Cloth, Uncut Edges and Gilt Tops, $7 00; Half Calf, $9 25. (In a Box.)

Caricature and other Comic Art,
In All Times and Many Lands. By James Parton. With 203 Illustrations. 8vo, Cloth, Gilt Tops and Uncut Edges, $5 00; Half Calf, $7 25.

The Ceramic Art:
A Compendium of the History and Manufacture of Pottery and Porcelain. By Jennie J. Young. With 464 Illustrations. 8vo, Cloth, $5 00.

Modern Dwellings in Town and Country,
Adapted to American Wants and Climate. In a Series of One Hundred Original Designs, comprising Cottages, Villas, and Mansions. With a Treatise on Furniture and Decoration. By H. Hudson Holly. 8vo, Cloth, $4 00.

Published by HARPER & BROTHERS, New York.

☞ Harper & Brothers *will send any of the above works by mail, postage prepaid, to any part of the United States, on receipt of the price.*

www.ingramcontent.com/pod-product-compliance
Lightning Source LLC
Chambersburg PA
CBHW031814220426
43662CB00007B/645